"Only the dea *the end of w*
(Attributed to) Plato

Walk with Warriors

Journey of Heroes

22 Veterans Share Their
Stories of Trials and
Triumphs

The editor mixed up my last name and my business name. 😊

Shannon Whittington

Walk with Warriors - Journey of Heroes
22 Veterans Share Their Stories of Trials and
Triumphs

ISBN: 978-0-692-91090-0

Military: Autobiography/Biography

INTRODUCTION

When the idea for this book first came to be, I was sitting in my living room talking with my husband about how I wanted to do something more meaningful for veterans. As we talked it through, my husband came up with the basis for this book: We would find veterans who were willing to share their story, and compile those stories into a single book. The idea was born!

I have been a patriot at heart for as long as I can remember. I won an award in 6th grade for writing an essay for the VFW about what the Constitution means to me. By my Junior year in high school, I knew I wanted to be a Navy fighter pilot. Unfortunately, life had other plans. Due to medical reasons, I was unable to fulfill that dream, but never lost heart for the men and women who serve, and have served, our great nation.

To have the honor to read these stories, and in some cases, coach these veterans through the emotions they endured while sharing their stories with you, means more to me than I could ever express.

My business is coaching people through the process of discovering and sharing their stories. This is difficult for most – excruciating for some of our veterans. However, what I had hoped for, and what

I have discovered in this process, is that writing is therapy. Having an outlet to pour out their long-held thoughts and emotions, to share them in a way that is safe, to help you to better understand the world they live in, internally, is therapy for these veterans.

There was no cost to any veteran who contributed to this book. This is our give-back to them. Our way of providing them an outlet, and letting them know someone cares! It is my hope, that as co-authors, you will begin seeing these veterans writing more, or even up on a stage, sharing their story to help others in their journeys.

I intentionally chose 22 veterans for this book. 22 veterans take their lives each day in America. That is 22 too many. It is my hope, that in sharing these stories, not only will these veterans find a weight lifted, but those who read these stories will come to know they are not alone. And for those of us who have never had to endure what our veterans have, it is my hope that we will come away with a better understanding and more compassion for our veterans. So that we can reach out, do our part, and turn that 22 to ZERO.

Thank you for reading their stories.

~ Shannon Whittington

Founder, Books By Vets

This book is dedicated to the 22.

"Not all wounds bleed externally."
Bernard Bergen, United States Army, Special
Forces

FORWARD

As veterans, we're a diverse bunch. Demographically, we're about as varied as the population we serve. We joined separate branches of the military and were trained in distinctive warfare specialties. We served in different eras and fought in different wars. Even individuals who took part in the same battles often have wildly different recollections of events. Attempting to describe a "typical" veteran is an exercise in futility – there is no such creature.

But there is one thing we share – military service changes us. When we leave for civilian life after 2 years or 20, we are no longer the same person we were when we joined. How we move forward is largely up to us. Our time in the military is but one phase of our lives and we choose what comes next. The challenge of finding our "fit" in civilian life is never easy and the journey is different for all of us. Sometimes it begins by simply telling our story.

This is mine.

I spent 21 years in the Navy doing the stuff of dreams – flying fighter jets in service to my country. Whether in peacetime or combat, I had absolute clarity of purpose and no doubt as to what was expected of me both as an officer and part of something much larger than myself. That certainty kept me on course even when faced with excruciating loss. It was the beacon that guided me when the world seemed to be coming apart all around. It gave my life purpose and meaning.

When I came home from Iraq in 2007 and took off my uniform for the last time, I felt as if I had lost both. Struggling to make sense of what I had experienced at war and stripped of my identity, I had no idea how to cope. Separated from my brothers and sisters-in-arms, I began to lose touch with the warrior I always believed myself to be. I grew distant from friends and family and alcohol became a frequent companion. Within a year, my marriage failed and I found myself left to raise three kids alone.

The kids were trying to deal with the legacy of war and divorce and turning to me to help make sense of things. They needed a strong, stable father who supported them with love and patience. Who they had was a man gripped by depression, frequently expressed as explosive anger, and often directed at them. Without my dad, who put his own retirement plans on hold to move in and help us pick up the pieces, I shudder to think how much more damage my behavior might have caused.

It took a particularly ugly incident of road rage, about 2 years after I returned home, to finally serve as the catalyst for change. On that day, my children were in the car with me when some anonymous man cut me off and I snapped. All the frustration, sadness, bitterness, and guilt surfaced at once and manifested as a blinding rage – focused like a laser beam on this man. I chased him to the next red light and jumped out of my car to confront him. His windows were rolled up and I saw him lock his doors as he stared at me with a mixture of confusion and alarm (in retrospect, I doubt he even realized he had cut me off).

As I stood in the middle of the intersection screaming like a maniac through his closed window, I thank God my own windows were rolled down. Because that allowed me to hear something from the back seat of my car that stopped me in my tracks – the sound of my kids crying. I turned towards them and saw my 8-year-old pleading through tears, "Please, Daddy, no".

In that moment, I felt like a monster – and realized just how completely I had lost my way. My rage vanished and I felt only shame.

I don't recall exactly what happened next. With the wind gone completely from my sails, I'm sure I muttered an apology of some kind and slinked back to my car. But I remember precisely what I did when I got home. I began searching on-line for counselors, both for myself and my kids.

That day turned out to be a pivot point in my life. I got help and gradually identified the cause of my depression as well as constructive ways to manage it. As my self-awareness deepened, the anger subsided and I found it easier to connect with others, especially my children. In time, I opened my heart to a very special woman who would later become my wife.

While I was working on my issues, my kids were seeing a counselor who specialized in equine therapy. I became fascinated with how horses helped them build self-esteem, understand their emotions, and learn to trust again. Their experience at the ranch proved transformative for all of us. It even inspired me to go back to school and get my Master's in counseling.

In school, I specialized in veterans' issues and animal assisted therapy (with an emphasis on equine therapy). Upon graduation, I took a position with a local nonprofit called Equest that was leveraging this unique style of therapy to help veterans and military families with their civilian transitions through a program they called "Hooves for Heroes".

I've been at Equest for 6 years now. In that time, I've worked with hundreds of veterans grappling with some of the same challenges I faced when I came home. For many of them and the families who love them, the horses provide unconditional acceptance and support while they attempt to answer tough questions. Questions about life and death; meaning and purpose; love and loss. Through the process, these men and women often discover the beacon that guides them is still there, only in a different guise; a new tribe awaits to help them on the journey; and the warrior is still very much alive in their hearts.

Through their healing, I've found renewed purpose.

When I was asked to write the forward for this book, I was excited to do it. I've always believed story-telling can help heal – but I had never really told my own, at least not all of it. As I write these words, it feels as if a weight has been lifted, even after all these years.

Meet 22 warriors with a story to tell. Their words will likely move and inspire you and you might even see pieces of yourself in these chapters. For the authors, this project can be an essential step in the journey of healing. Simply by capturing our stories in narrative form we start to make sense of the experiences we've had. By telling them to those willing to listen, we find common ground and shared humanity - and a connection that can make all the difference.

Jeff Hensley, United States Navy, Retired

ALLEN SHELL
United States Army

I had always thought that if I ever got a chance to write a book, I knew what the first paragraph would say. Beyond that, I guess I don't have a clue. When you talk about your "PTSD" that's digging into the depths of areas that most of the populous either doesn't have any business knowing, or as it seems at times, "That's just another crazy Veteran that's gone off the deep end." You're right! Hopefully I can relay my path or way ahead out of the dark and it can help drag you to the light. Have I figured out the Holy Grail or found the Fountain of Youth and cure-all approach? Hell no! To be totally honest, none of us will ever be totally cured. We deal with a million different things and all we can ever hope for is the ability to find peace and find a way to quell the demons that live in us. It's not a "poof" and you're good to go. It's a never-ending path, but with the help of others and your faith, you find a way to meet in the middle in agreement with the past. Remember, look forward. I always tell my kids that your windshield of your car is much bigger than the rearview mirror looking backward. We must focus on always trudging ahead. You can't forget the past, but it should not determine who you are or dictate your path forward.

I saw this quote awhile back on Pinterest and said, "That would make an awesome quote!" It hit the nail on the head and probably describes 98% of all of us that are reading this chapter. "I like to burn my bridges while I'm standing on them so people know I'm serious about my crazy." Powerful statement. Of course, it fell under the column of Burning Bridge Quotes and the Humor section. The funny thing was, I was serious. Focusing on the real meaning of this simple quote, I rationalized who I now was. I had become the asshole I always talked about not being. I had become the self-destructive person that hurt those around me and didn't have a foggy clue as to who I had become. I rode my Harley-Davidson at 70mph on the exit ramps and curves and I snuck alcohol out of the liquor cabinet and casually mixed it with prescribed narcotics with little to no inclination of the dangerous path I was going down. The thing was, I also didn't give a damn what others thought or how it affected others.

I won't bore the masses with my life story of how I got where I was at in life. That's probably one of the biggest turn-off's when I read any of the "How To" books from the 50lb brain thinkers describing the multiple degrees they have and things they have done that qualify them to rate my experience or fix my issues. I've done it all…the breathing exercises, relaxation sessions and soft music while sitting in the Laz-Y-Boy recliner at the post-deployment health clinic. I've been tossed out of support groups because I was argumentative and have trolled around for years trying to find my fix. I think what truly scared the hell out of me was how drastically changed your inner self can turn. When you can walk past something so horrific that it would make a grown man lose his stomach and it doesn't even phase you and you can sleep well at night…you're forever changed. You just established a new standard. This isn't a normal standard either.

My quick background. I was born into an upper-middle class family in Laurens, South Carolina in 1965. I guess you can say it was a large family by today's standards. I was the fourth out of four kids. I had two older sisters and an older brother. Just for comparison in age, my older sister was twelve years older than me and my older brother was almost seven years my senior. It was kind of cool because I could say I was from a large family but with the span in age, I lived the hellacious life of an only child. My parents were from the Greatest Generation. They were both raised during the Depression and my father was a veteran from the Pacific in World War II and was a Chief Petty Officer in the U.S. Navy. If you ask me who the smartest man I ever met in my life was, it would be my father. The funny thing, he never finished high school. He went to work in my grandfather's grocery store back in Laurens after he knew the basics of reading, writing and arithmetic. I don't care what education I ever had behind me, that man could easily run circles around my young mind with both eyes closed. As I know now, he suffered from PTSD as a result of his experiences fighting in the Pacific. We would talk at length, even in the days when he suffered from Alzheimer's, with great clarity about his experiences. To be truthful, some of his stories scared the hell out of me. They still do. It wasn't called PTSD then, and was carried as excess baggage and wasn't discussed like it is today. My mother was the recipient of many nightmares and other associated symptoms.

I attended The Citadel. The Military College of South Carolina is in Charleston, South Carolina. I graduated in 1988 and received my commission as a 2LT in the U.S. Army as a Field Artillery officer. It's comical why I even ended up at The Citadel. My family had deep roots at Clemson University. My mother worked as a legal secretary for the Clemson Alumni and Chairman of the Board of Visitors for Clemson, Paul W. McAlister. I was raised in the same church and when it came time to go to college, it was assumed that I would go where most of the family attended. You could have heard a pin drop when I went against the grain and said I was going to Charleston. As a matter of fact, I only applied to The Citadel and no other schools. Honoring Mr. McAlister's wishes, I attended a college visit at Clemson my senior year in high school. That was a funny story. I showed up to the alumni office, IPTAY, as it was called. That stood for "I Pay Thirty a Year" which was the school alumni association. As with most schools, I bet alumni pay more than $30 a year now. Anyway, I digress. I showed up at my appointed time and hands-down, one of the most beautiful girls I had ever seen showed up to give me my campus tour. I am still not sure what it is about girls and white shorts, but I did my duty and completed my college tour. They really rolled out the red carpet to say the least. Anyway, I met up with my father at the end of the day and asked him the million-dollar question after he asked me how I enjoyed the tour. "Pop, is it true that you promised each of us kids four years of college?" My father had guaranteed that all his kids would get four years of school since he never had the opportunity during the Depression. He answered, "Yes, that's still the case. How'd you like your tour?" My answer I gave him was probably one of those divine intervention moments that forever affected my life path. I told my father, "Pop, if you're only giving me four years, it will take me ten years to get out of this place. I'm going to The Citadel."

Let's fast forward for the sake of time. A 21-year career with my beautiful wife and high school sweetheart and four awesome kids. I was, as I had been in school and growing up, the practical joker and took absolutely nothing serious. I must applaud my wife, Lilliana, in that she was a true champion. She endured many deployments, field exercises, and associated TDY's while I was never there. And when I was there, I ended up being the fifth child. The family is the foundation for everything that we are and have been next to our good Lord above. My family was no different. Lilliana was and is my champion, cheerleader, fixer and the best Chief of Staff I could have ever asked for in a wife. She never asked for this life, and hindsight being 20/20, she probably never would have ventured down that path again for any amount of money in the world. At the end of the day, the family is the silent victim when it comes to the wounds of war. My great family is no different. Writing my story, I had to dig back into my memories of my father and his decline with Alzheimer's. In many ways, PTSD and Alzheimer's share many similarities. I don't mean the disease itself, but how those around ultimately pay the price and suffer as the casualties in the wake of the symptoms from the disease. If I have learned anything from going down the path of both ailments, it's that those closest to the patient are usually the ones that take the brunt of the abuse. I was no different. I can go down the laundry list and many veterans will check the items off in your head and say, "Yep, I've done that!" I was withdrawn, my spontaneity of humor was gone and I could go from zero to sixty in a moment's notice with my temper and I didn't care who caught the brunt of my tirade. To be totally blunt, I was that asshole I said I would never be.

After my last tour to Iraq as a commander of a Brigade Military Transition Team (MiTT) during the Surge from 2007-2008, I decided it was time to throw in the towel and retire. After 21 years in uniform, I was burned out and ready for the next chapter in my life. I wanted predictability and to hang out with the kids, go to the Friday night football games and go fishing with the boys on Saturdays. I think that's all us as warrior's want after running at full speed for so long...normalcy. After trying to get back to my normalcy back at Fort Sill upon returning from OIF was a challenge to say the least. I thought I was doing okay, but that's the funny thing with PTSD. You don't realize how you react or appear to the general public. I thought I was cruising along, business as usual and good-to-go. My boss at the time, COL(Ret) Frank Siltman, was the Director of Training and Doctrine (DOTD) at Fort Sill. He welcomed me back to DOTD and was about one of the best bosses you could work for in the Army. He eased me back into the work environment of TRADOC at the Field Artillery School and he always told me, "Allen, take what time you need to get back into the swing of things." He would come back later and say, "Allen, you got back to work fairly quick, are you sure you don't need more time to get back into the mix?" Of course, my answer was always, "I'm fine. Why do you ask?" It is LTC(Ret) David Henderson I attribute with pulling my butt out of the fire. Dave was the Deputy Director under COL Siltman and was already a former battalion commander that had retired from the Army and was serving as a DA-Civilian in the Deputy DOTD slot. He is a Christian and I had daily interaction with him in my job at DOTD. He essentially gets the credit with saving my sanity and helping me see who I had become. I'll never forget the exchange. "Allen, how are you doing?" I answered, "Fine Dave, why do you ask?" Dave didn't beat around the bush. He point-blank spelled it out for me without beating around the bush. "Allen, I think you need help, and how is your life as a Christian?" What the hell! I was dumbfounded. Why would anyone ask me that? That initial "in your face" moment started my path to acceptance and path forward to fixing my jacked-up life. Dave didn't let me wander, but kept me on the glidepath. He knew I would blow him off, and he set up an appointment for me with the team at the Post-Deployment Mental Health Clinic on post. That was an experience in itself. I walk in for my appointment and they give me the old dreaded 100 question survey that we've all filled out. You know the one, "Do you feel like hurting yourself or others?" and all that crap. As I sat there, I started to look around and thought to myself, "I'm not crazy, why in the hell am I here sitting with a bunch of poo-nanny pscycho's filling out a stupid ass questionnaire?" Well, that questionnaire apparently didn't score well, as I was told, and I got stuck in the short line and told to fill out more paperwork. I won myself an actual sit-down with a genuine shrink. After many sessions, I came to the realization that all was not well in the Land of Oz. I needed help. I still remember, the Doctor actually came over to me after clapping his hands in support and he patted me on the back and said, "Allen, I'm proud of you. 99.9% of the battle is admitting you have a problem. You did that, and I'm proud of you." Yeah, that moment was also one of those divine intervention moments you don't forget.

Dave stayed in my knickers regarding my way ahead. That was both awkward and infuriating at the same time for me. Why the hell would someone take the time, energy and effort to be involved with not only my mental health, but my spiritual well-being? Trust me, I skirted those conversations every chance I got. Dave was persistent and dogged with his approach. I'd go to a meeting with him on some project I was working on and damn if he had me hostage and would ask, "Allen, how's your relationship with God?" Go to hell Dave, why would you ask me that? I was running, and running scared. The demons were biting at my heels and I couldn't escape. It was that same uncomfortable place all of us have been that you wish you were a million miles away and not where you were sitting. Damn! I figured, meet this monster head-on. "Dave, I don't go to church. I am a Christian." Dave would then ask, "Why don't you go to church? I know going to church doesn't make you a Christian, but you need that foundation to help you heal." Oh yeah, now I have the spiritual healing thing to worry about. I'm crazy and now people want Christ to fix me. I can't escape this madness. I blurted it out and was as direct as I knew how in my response. "Dave, I'm not worthy of going to church. I'm not worthy of being called a Christian. I have done things, seen things and participated in things that will never be forgiven and I am not worthy to enter the house of God. Leave me alone..." Dave interrupted me, "Allen, none of us have clean feet and none of us are worthy. The door to the church goes both ways and God never said we had to be perfect. I'm not and you're not." I lost it. Never had I had something so simple explained in a way that would affect me like a blinding flash. That was another one of those divine intervention moments I keep telling you about. If you haven't figured it out, those moments aren't arbitrary or by accident. Whether you figure it out from me explaining my path ahead, or somebody has to draw you a picture in crayon, the Lord above is driving this bus and you're only the occupant. Take off your bus driver's hat and get out of the driver's seat, because you're not in charge Buddy!

Let's talk more about that destructive behavior I seem to have down like a pro. Yes, my loving wife deserves the credit for keeping the whole family functioning and together. It all seems one-sided now when I look back. I left her holding the bag while I deployed, with four young kids, and left her holding the bag when I got back as well. Some deal, isn't it? She got us all back into church and I felt better. I was missing something. Aside from the mental scars I was dealing with, I also had some physical scars that I brought home from Iraq. I had damaged nerves, my back was a wreck and I, like most of us, couldn't sleep. This along with the visits to mental health and the narcotics opened another realm of "Jacked Up" that I never knew existed. I took the drugs to help me sleep and when I hit what was a REM cycle of real sleep, the demons that I had managed to keep at bay would come out to play at night. Damned if you do, and damned if you don't. Get sleep to help on one side, and the bad guys come out to wreak havoc. At what cost, and where is the middle ground? That had me sneaking booze out of the liquor cabinet and mixing that with the drugs just to find peace and some middle ground. Talk about a dangerous combination. I was always angry, I was always irritable. I alienated my best friend and beautiful wife, and I was horrible to my kids. I can remember one night in the kitchen, I destroyed both of my daughter's. The questions will always come. We've all had them, "What are some war stories from Iraq?" "Did you kill anybody?" "Tell me about some of the cool stuff you did." At that time, at that moment, I unleashed the years of pain, aggression and built-up hate and memories. All in that moment, my two beautiful girls were the recipients of something they never deserved. They would be forever scarred with the onslaught of all that hate that had built up and turned loose on their innocence at such a simple question asked by a child that was curious. What destroyed me that night and helped me realize, I was not that wonderful father and knight in shining armor standing on a pedestal that was a perfect example of what a father should be in a child's eyes. I was evil, I was hateful and something that was not worthy to be called "Daddy". Something died in me that night and I never could find it. It was gone. I'm still trying to find that part of me.

I guess all my wayward ways caught up with me over Christmas 2016. The circumstances aren't important, but everything came to a head. I did what I never intended on doing. I hurt the people that loved me most. I broke them. Just like the rough surf constantly hitting the rocks over the years, it gradually wears them down. I did that to my best friend, my high school sweetheart, my Princess...Lilliana. The day in and day out trudging along, just getting by, and constant band-aid approach took its toll. When she was at the end of her rope and threw out the lifeline, I let her falter and almost drown. My faults and chinks in my armor almost destroyed the one thing that has been constant in my life. If you remember from the start of this chapter, I said that the one thing we as warriors desire is peace and normalcy. Lilliana provided that peace and normalcy and had been my security for all these years. She was my constant and my stability. PTSD had broken me and almost destroyed my life with the one true champion that had stood by my side. This is the path of destruction that I finally realized and had to face. I don't have all the answers, but the moment you realize and wake the hell up and figure out that those closest to you are the key and your faith in the good Lord above, you can re-build the foundation that has crumbled.

I'm reminded of the movie Forrest Gump when I think of PTSD Support Groups. You're probably thinking I have lost my freaking mind. What the heck does this movie have to do with PTSD. Focus with me for a second. Look at the path that Gary Sinise took as he played LT Dan Taylor in that movie. I've met Gary. He has probably done more for veterans and our cause than any other celebrity out there. He's a great American! When you go back to that movie at the end, Forrest explains that LT Dan "made his peace with God". No matter what our path, all we ever are trying to do is find that middle ground. I don't have the answers, just like none of us do. What I can say, is that all we are trying to achieve is that inner peace so we can move ahead. Stop looking in the rearview mirror. Look forward and don't travel alone. I know that has made all the difference.

BILL BRANCH
United States Navy

My name is E.J. Branch and I am a Navy veteran. I joined the Navy in January of 1951 out of Lindsay, OK—just a farm boy. I was 19 years old and my brother, Bill, who was 18, followed me the next day. I got Sid Smith, who is the grocery man here, to enlist with me. The three of us went through boot camp together in San Diego in 1951 and I had an interesting career.

I'd like to tell you a story about my brother who was a Bo'sun's mate and a coxswain that ran LCBP small boats. In all due respect, he didn't go to school because they didn't want to mess him up—he was good immediately with the small boat, and he was the captain's personal favorite pushing the boat in a tight spot. We were operating in an LST—a landing ship that had a tank deck and a main deck. It carries tanks, equipment, troops. The doors opened to drop the ramp from the main deck—the doors on the ship beach it, and the stern anchor pulls you away from the beach. That's how you get off the beach. We lost a part, and the doors were inoperable. We were in 18 feet of water, and they asked for volunteers to go down and see if they could locate the shoe. They wanted to tie a line on it and pull it up. If not, we would have to salvage our operation and go back to a port to get the ship repaired.

A boy named Fred Curtis went down, but he couldn't stay down long enough. Bill was the other one that volunteered and he went down and located it, but he had to have air so he came back. It was against regulations to do that without headgear and without any protection. Bill came back up and said he could find it, but he couldn't stay down long enough. They said, "Well, we'll have to get the frogmen." So, he said, "Give me some weight to hold on to and get me down quicker." And he had a line to tie to the shoe. So, they got him a weight, 25 or 30 pounds. He was 5 feet 10 inches tall and weighed 175 pounds, in perfect shape. So, this weight calmed him down quicker, and he could stay under water a long time, more than average. So, he went down and tied this knot around this deal and they pulled the shoe up. When came up, it was quite a deal. He got a captain's commendation for that. He was fine afterwards, but he started having problems with his ears because of the pressure. They sent him to the hospital and they examined him. My captain came to me, he was a couple of years from retirement. He called me over and said, "Don't write home about Bill. I'd like you to keep this to yourself. He should have had headgear. I'll take care of Bill." So, I said, "I'm not very good about writing home about anything. I don't bother my mother with anything pertaining to business." From then on, any request I requested was granted, and we went on a couple more years.

Bill had problems with his ears. They wanted to discharge him, but he tore the discharge papers up and threw them over the side because he wanted to stay with me. He and I made two trips to Korea and back during our time. We spent all of 1952 there, and we saw combat. I got a Korean medal with two battle stars. Our LST was picked to load Seabees and equipment on a mission to go to Wonsan, Korea, and build an emergency landing strip. We went in there June 1952, and we had 500 barrels of fuel on the main deck, chained down, for fuel for the operation. We got to our destination, which was a hot spot, and the USS Iowa was our backup—the big battleship equal to the Missouri. It was shelling destroyers and aircraft carriers. We lost ship's power drifting in to the beach to unload. We dropped the ramp to unload the fuel, but we didn't get plumb into the beach because we lost power. So, we used manual steering, but we couldn't get any further and we dropped the ramp. Half the crew got in the water, and the other half walked the barrels down the ramp. A barrel that's 45 or 50% full will float, and we pushed the barrels to shore under the enemy's nose. They fired on us, but they didn't hit us. The landing strip was completed in 30 days. It was for crippled planes to land—rather than hit the water or be captured, they would hit that emergency strip and a helicopter would pick them up. In fact, they opened the strip before it was completed, and three pilots hit there and got saved the first day.

The story of this operation was told in a newspaper article, "*One Ship 'Fleet' at P.H. After Secret Mission:* A one shop invasion "fleet" is at Pearl Harbor after completing a secret operation against the Communists in Wonsan Harbor.

The "fleet" is the LST 692, a Navy landing craft that made an amphibious landing in the north Korean harbor, ringed on three sides by coastal defense guns of the Communists.

Protected by the 16 inch rifles of the battleship Iowa and the guns of other Allied warships, LST 692 accomplished her mission and escaped with no casualties, although shrapnel from the near misses sprayed her decks.

So successful was the operation, the Navy said, that the landing craft could pause long enough to rescue a downed carrier pilot, who crashed near the ship."

Beyond those sketchy details, the Navy would not elaborate on the operation, which earned the landing craft a commendation from the Commander of Naval Forces in the Far East for "resourcefulness and efficiency."

Described as "one of the Navy's most versatile ships," the LST 692 was also used for anti-invasion patrol of the islands off the coast

In one action, a patrol boat carrying men of the U.S. Navy and Royal British Marines was lost. The LST 692 arrived on a Saturday, in company with LST 914, and the landing craft repair ship Atlas. The three ships would leave the following day for the West Coast.

We also did a little tour of Vietnam in 1954 when France fell to Vietnam. France got whipped and they sent my ship up the river because it was a flat-bottomed ship and we could move the French survivors and the equipment out of there. We went into Haiphong Harbor, but it does not show on our record that we were ever there because we were not supposed to be there. But I have slides and pictures.

I boxed on that LST. I had fun. We were on that ship 44 months— it was my home, and my brother's home. We were never separated. I have great memories of that experience. We came home in 1952, and I got a baseball tryout and they transferred us—I talked them into taking Bill, too—to Coronado, headquarters for the amphibious fleet in San Diego. We played baseball for three months and then went back to the ship and went back over. I pitched and Bill caught. Bill and I are 19 months apart and are as close as two brothers can get. He was a topnotch sailor—he looked like one, and he was not as mischievous as I was. I got the good conduct medal, but I was about half outlaw to tell the truth. In those days, we scrapped a lot.

In 1954, in the fall just before my brother and I got out, we were coming back in from Vietnam into the South China Straits and we got in a typhoon. The weather reports weren't as accurate as they are now, and at 7.3 we couldn't outrun it, so we couldn't get away from it. We were in it six days and six nights and it did severe damage to our ship. In fact, it wouldn't have lasted one more day. Horrible looking angry seas. If a man falls overboard, he's gone. The waves were huge. You have to go right into them—if you get into a trough, it will flip you over. We didn't make any headway—we just floundered. You had to strap yourself in the bunk, and when you went to eat you had to hold your arm on a tray of food because the tray would go high. The cook would get down in the galley and he couldn't get up—he would slide. The grates on the galley ranges blew and the seams in the bulkhead, they went to crackin'. When we limped in and got out of it, everyone was real grateful. It was probably the toughest duty we had all the time I was in. They had to put a complete undercarriage on that ship. It wouldn't have lasted very long. The shipyard put a whole metal plate under the whole bottom of the ship before we could come home. The ship was donated to the Philippine Navy LST 692. Anyone that ever rode out a typhoon will know what I'm talking about.

A lot of people were sad to see us go when we got out of the Navy. We had a ship's party in 1954 just before I got out. The last one we'd had was in 1952 in Vallejo, California, and it was a wreck; a lot fights and I was in on some of them. So, we didn't have another one until 1954, and for that one they appointed me to shore patrol. There was talk they were going to whip one of the chief petty officers, and the captain gave me orders for shore patrol and told me to eliminate all fights. He said, "Get you another man or two. You walk around. You don't drink. You be all business, and those are your orders. There's talk they're going to jump on Chief Gary. My orders to you are don't let that happen." And I looked straight at him and told him I would not let that happen. It was a pretty good evening, and I didn't drink because I had my orders. I picked me another couple of guys and it started to break out on Gary and I stopped it. I had a way about me that I stopped it. I had a pretty good reputation as being pretty good with my fists. So, there wasn't any trouble, and the captain introduced me to some other captains who were guests. He said, "This boy Branch is a baseball pitcher. I want to challenge you to baseball game." We never did play the game, though. We were also told, "Do not bother the captain for overnight liberty. Do not bother the captain or any officer." So, I walked over to the captain just to see if l could do it after I had averted all the trouble. And I said, "Captain, I'd like to have an overnight pass." And he got a napkin (I wish I still had that napkin!) and he gave me a 72-hour pass, written right on that napkin.

I don't want to portray myself as a hero, but I'm proud of my service. I did some things in the line of duty, but others have done much more. Audie Murphy was a hero. The Pearson brothers were genuine heroes. A.B. Pearson told me a story — he was a great baseball player and he was always big. Billy Conn fought Joe Lewis for the heavyweight championship of the world in the early 1940s. Billy Conn was a light heavyweight champion who went up a weight to heavyweight, and he fought Joe Lewis to the 13th round and had 11 out of the 13 rounds won. Conn was going to put on an exhibition to entertain the troops in England. They wanted some big guy to work out Conn a little with headgear on, and they didn't have anyone except A.B., but he was in the brig — he was kind of a bandit. So, they told A.B. they'd get him out of the brig if he'd work out with Billy Conn. He got suited up, put the headgear on and they sparred. When it was over A.B. said, "We were sparring there and I took bad aim at him with a haymaker and he sure did punish me!"

After the military, I came back to Oklahoma. I got married, I farmed a year and won enough money shooting dice to get me a truck and went to hauling gravel. As time went on, I developed a company, and in 10 or 12 years I had my own company. I had my trucking company about 30 years. I ran race horses, too. I've lived a full life; a life I've enjoyed. I've had my share of trouble, but I've had a lot of fun. I've helped a lot of people along the way.

During his life after his military service, my brother, Bill Branch, served three terms as sheriff of Garvin County.

Let those who know not how to pray go to sea.

BRYAN TILOS
United States Navy

They say when adversity occurs, your character is being tested. I honestly believe that trials and challenges are needed so that we can grow and become stronger. There comes a time in our life when we ask what the purpose of our life is. Every day, we are bombarded by circumstances that we cannot control and it is up to us to decide how we will react to them. On that fateful date of March 11, 2011, a powerful 8.8 magnitude shook mainland Japan and a devastating 15-meter tsunami followed shortly after causing massive damage and thousands of casualties. My life changed and the events that occurred in Japan have deeply impacted on how I view my life today.

This is my story...

March 10, 2011

I was a Second Lieutenant in the United States Air Force, stationed in Yokota Air Base, Japan. The base had undergone an exercise called an ORE (Operational Readiness Exercise). This is like a base-wide inspection and inspectors grade us to see if we can perform under austere conditions. I remember it was a cool week with weather ranging in the 70s-80s. I was in charge of an Aircraft Maintenance Squadron and scheduled for graveyard shift from 6pm – 6am. It was about 5am and it was almost time for shift change. I just ate my last snack; a delicious peanut butter protein bar.

It was still dark as I headed into our work building where I gave aircraft statuses to the shift supervisors. For a week straight, the base participated in an exercise where we had to wear chemical gear, a flak vest, reflective gear, a flak helmet, and over-sized rubber boots. I'd say I was wearing an extra 20 pounds of gear. Boy, it was heavy. I was ready to go home and sleep.

I didn't live too far away from the base. As soon as I parked in my small driveway, I got my bag full of uniforms and walked upstairs to my house. It was around 6:10 am and I was half awake. I was exhausted. I watched a little bit of TV, and fell asleep shortly after.

March 11, 2011

It was approximately 1:30 pm and I woke up feeling refreshed. I got up to check my e-mail, went on Facebook and scrolled through my news feed while eating 7-11 sushi. After eating and doing my daily activities, I decided to call my family back in Washington State. I had Vonage, which allowed me to use my internet to call local numbers in the U.S. using my landline. It was a neat feature. It was around 1:45pm my time, and I called my sister Jennifer in Washington (9:45pm PST). We talked for 40 minutes when suddenly I felt this intense shaking and swaying. I lived on the second story of a quad-plex and I felt the building was going to collapse.

I was literally freaking out. It lasted for 30-45 seconds, but felt like 2-3 minutes. My sister asked, "Are you okay?" I nervously responded, "Yeah, I think we had an earthquake! Man, that was intense and strong!" I briefly talked to my mom for a bit and let her know that I was okay.

I hung up the phone and tried to call my boss via cell phone. My cell phone wasn't working. Hmm, I tried a couple more times. Still, nothing going through. The cell phone towers were affected. The connection was lost and I was still figuring out what was happening. Then it hit me as I turned on my TV, watching the local Japanese channels – we'd just had an 8.8 magnitude earthquake!

Fortunately, my internet was working and I logged onto Facebook and saw a slew of messages about the huge shaking. I updated my Facebook status as "Hey everybody, I'm doing fine and survived that massive earthquake". I was watching the local Japanese news at the time, and the center of the earthquake was located just outside Sendai, Japan; approximately 100 miles away. Then, I saw something on TV that I'll never forget – a tsunami heading towards the shores of Sendai. I couldn't believe my eyes.

At that very moment, I was shocked, scared, and confused. It all happened at once. I prayed and asked God to help us. We needed it...badly. As I glued my eyes to my TV screen, all I saw was a rush of water sweeping the town and thousands of people being washed away. I quickly turned away and tried not to break down. I had to keep it together because I know emotions can take over a human very quickly. I told myself, "Bryan, you got to keep it together! You're a US Air Force Officer and your role is to stay calm and focus on the mission. God will take care of this."

Minutes later, I got a call from my Commander. "Lieutenant Tilos, are you okay?" I said softly, "Yes, Sir, I'm doing fine. I can't believe that tsunami washed up so many people". My Commander said, "Yeah, I know, but we have a mission to do. We are to serve and help those in need in the affected areas. I want you to report at the base ASAP and we will give further instructions. Understood?" "Yes, Sir!" I said while I stood up. I quickly changed into my uniform, went downstairs, hopped into my car and headed towards the base.

As I was driving, there were so many thoughts that were racing through my mind. I looked around the local area and saw the faces of the Japanese people. They were so calm, so relaxed; as if the Tsunami didn't affect them. It was about a ten-minute drive to my work. When I arrived, our commander had a meeting in the auditorium and advised us on what happened. A lot of us were still confused and still didn't know all the details. All I knew is that we had to save those being affected. I looked around and saw many of my fellow Airmen ready to accomplish the mission. That was our focus. Everybody depended on us to ensure the aircraft was ready to fly.

My commander pulled me aside and gave me the run down on what needed to be done. I looked at him, acknowledged his response and got to work. "All right guys, this is going to be our task – we need to relocate our items from this building to building 3 on the other side of the base." All the maintenance personnel took chairs, desks, tables, tools, and computers to haul to the other side. It all seemed like a blur but we had a mission to complete. The Japanese community depended on us.

Since this was a humanitarian relief mission, the base commander decided to call the task, Operation Tomodachi. The word Tomodachi means "Friendship" in Japanese. The Japanese community (and the rest of Japan) depended our base to operate with mission-ready aircraft to drop off supplies to the affected area.

It took about three hours to move our belongings to the other side. It was at this very moment I had to keep myself in check. I knew that I had a responsibility and it was time for me to set the example. All I could think about were the affected Japanese people being swept and washed away by the devastating tsunami. When we got our items completely moved to the building, we ensured we had all the tools and supplies we needed. We were working 12-hour shifts, 6-days, with 1 day off during the week.

My main task as a Maintenance Officer was to make sure the aircraft were ready to fly. All I could think about were the lives that we needed to save. I knew that I had to keep our morale up and be ready for any sudden changes. Well, there was another surprise – because of the 8.8 magnitude earthquake, the nuclear reactors were affected. Yes, radiation was being exposed and we were 143 miles from it. Last thing on my mind was the radiation exposure. I could see it all over the news. Following a major earthquake, a 15-meter tsunami disabled the power supply and cooling of three Fukushima Daiichi reactors, causing a nuclear accident

"Lieutenant Tilos, I want you to ensure our aircraft is ready for the air crew. We need to ensure that all of the inspections have been completed and we have the necessary tools to service them" my Commander briefed me while I was in his office.

"Yes, Sir, copy that. You can count on me." I said proudly as I shook my Commander's hand.

I was pumped. This was it. I had the sudden realization on my current situation. Flashbacks came to me as I thought about my training in college, but also my life circumstances growing up. It was at this very moment that I was ready for this. Timing couldn't have been better. Deep down inside, I knew that my purpose was deepened. Not only was I an Air Force Officer, I also had to be strong and lead others so they would believe everything was going to be all right. All my life, I've always wanted to have the "I want to make a difference in someone's life" mentality. Here it was; my opportunity to shine and the whole world was looking at us to help.

Our C-130 aircraft were being flown every day to deliver supplies to the affected area in Sendai. We delivered around 1000+ pounds of aid daily. Every day, our tasks were to make sure the aircraft was being serviced. It was about three weeks since the devastation, and the local Japanese were being taken care of.

One story I recall was when a 70+ year-old Japanese man was stranded on top of a tree and below was the rush of water. One of our fellow maintainers knew how to fluently speak Japanese and was tasked to help the man. The maintainer rode in a helicopter with the search and rescue crew to the site. They put the maintainer on a hoist so that they could lower him to speak with the Japanese man. The man was comforted because the maintainer could speak Japanese. The maintainer told him that they were saving him from being stranded. He was so relieved and happy. The maintainer got a hold of him and hoisted him up with the assistance of the aircrew.

Another story was when the nuclear reactor was acting up. The Japanese military needed to cool down the reactor with a big fire hose. Well, there was a metal fitting that they needed, but didn't have. They requested the Australian Air Force to send theirs, but unfortunately it did not fit. The Australian Air Force called our base and we had the capability to cut the metal fitting to make it fit to the hose. It was a true victory when it happened. All I remember is that a crew of four – two eighteen year olds, one 25-year-old, and 27-year old, were in charge of a large task from the United States Air Force. They worked 12-hour days for 2 weeks and miraculously, it worked. The four-star General heard about their efforts and visited their workspace. He congratulated them by giving them his General coin. From that day, our base was recognized for a huge accomplishment and our morale was boosted.

As the weeks went by, I took a deep breath and realized that we got through the hard part. I accepted the natural disasters and the lives lost. Day in and day out, we would send water and food to the affected areas via aircraft transportation. I looked around my squadron and could tell things were going to be all right. We had other military bases that were leaning on us to succeed. And boy, we were going to be the best here on out!

It was about one month in, and the situation started to stabilize. We went from working six days a week, to five days. We realized that that life was getting back to its normal routine. I was relieved on much work was being put into the mission. The community of Yokota Air Base, and the local Japanese, worked closer than ever. I could see the strengthening of the ties between them.

Here are a few lessons I learned from this whole, chaotic experience:

1) <u>Keep Perspective</u> – In the midst of the tsunami and ensuring the job is getting done, it is important to maintain perspective and know everything is going to work out. It's easy to get caught up in the moment and derail

yourself, which will cause you to be unfocused. Remind yourself to stay the path and get the job done.

2) <u>Attitude is Everything</u> – This is easier said than done. When the media inundated me, I had to complete 10 things at once. This was a challenge. I had to make sure my attitude was in check. I did my very best not to complain, and I had to be the encourager to my team and organization.

3) <u>Be grateful</u> – I had to be grateful that I had an opportunity to help others on a bigger scale. I would have never thought I would be in a situation where the base I was stationed at was the central hub for all the operations. At times, I had to stop and tell myself that I am grateful to aid others so I can learn from this.

4) <u>Appreciate the small things</u> – It's important to look over the small things because at the time, they seemed insignificant. Whether it's a smile, or a pat on the back, I knew that I had to appreciate what happened daily.

I was thankful for the experience in Japan for all it taught me. It helped me become a stronger person. I knew that during the chaos, the situation was going to improve and we, as a community, were going to be stronger than ever.

As I reflect the events that occurred 5 years ago, I will never forget the friendships that were made after the situation. I constantly remind myself to appreciate the small things in life. When a trial comes into my life, I know that I should remain calm and encourage others to look up. Time and time again, I am put into positions where I must lead others and be an example. Operation Tomodachi has taught me so many valuable lessons, including the resilience of the Japanese community. They held their heads up and kept on smiling. I know that when I saw their faces, there was hope. I am truly thankful to have matured as a leader and as a person overall.

EDDIE PENNEY
United States Navy

I was approached about this project from an extremely important person to me; a very dear friend. He explained it was to show how PTSD affects veterans based on certain experiences we are exposed to and often fall victim to. Good news...we can overcome any issues that we experienced in the military and throughout life. I'd like to share a few of my personal struggles to provide hope to fellow service members and man alike. I was very hesitant about doing this because I am not one that likes to "story tell," but with the rate of veteran suicide gaining momentum, I thought, if I could just help one person from taking his or her life, that it would be more than worth it.

My military career is full of pride and honor to serve the greatest country in the world. If you do not believe that statement, then please visit other countries. You'll see I speak the truth.

I started my military career in 1996 by enlisting in the Marine Corps as an infantryman. I was 17. I quickly realized that the US military was not the same as what I imagined or saw in the movies. It was real life and there was blood, sweat and tears. Gone were the days of lounging on a couch, eating popcorn and thinking about how awesome it would be to fight the enemy.

The Marine lifestyle was great and I learned a lot, but there was something I was missing. I had a greater calling.

I switched services and joined the Navy to become a Navy SEAL. Making the switch was an easy call because I wanted to be at the "tip of the spear" and get as much combat action as possible.

Just like the movies, right? Wrong.

I was focused. I was determined. I knew that if I did not make the Teams, I would be like the other hundreds of candidates who didn't make it and would have to go to the Fleet Navy (which was the LAST thing I wanted to do). I knew I would succeed, and so – I did.

I completed training and went to SEAL Team 2, where I did two combat deployments in both Iraq and Afghanistan. Upon my return from my second deployment, I screened and was picked up for Naval Special Warfare Development Group (NSWDG/SEAL Team 6). Upon my completion of training, I was assigned to a squadron and began my first workup to head back over to Iraq.

Being at SEAL Team 2 and SEAL Team 6 are two very different worlds. I loved them both and have nothing but respect for the brave men that serve for them and truly make a difference.

The difference between each Team is the level of risk that you are involved with. At Team 6, the targets are way more aggressive with the shootings and explosions. Death is a nightly occurrence. The only way to deal with this is to stuff it down deep inside and carry on with the task at hand. There is no time to think, and less time feel. If you allow yourself those luxuries, you are not doing what you are supposed to be doing: taking the fight to the enemy and ridding their evil deeds from this earth.

I'm convinced that the reason I made it through training, after all the physical strain and mental tests, was due to my ability to separate my feelings from the job. But, the emotional build up has a price.

That price comes very fast and without warning.

I did a total of 7 deployments, all to combat areas, and loved every moment of them all. Bringing justice and ridding terrorists from this world is an indescribable feeling that never gets old. As with anything, good often comes with bad. Unfortunately, in this line of work the bad is life ending. There were times where I had my dearest friends next to me alive and well, and then the very next moment they are gone. No good-byes and no last words. The fog of war is very real, and for me, stuffing all the sadness and hurt is the way I dealt with it for years and years. We all did. I am not alone on this at all.

I know many who read this know exactly what I am talking about. It does not mean you are weak, it only means you are human. We were all made to feel.

Losing a beloved friend did something to me; it made me very cold and calloused. I honestly did not realize it at the time. I went from a somewhat normal man to a stone-cold operator. I lost a lot of feelings and emotions and channeled all my built-up anger and aggression to our enemies. Callousness happens when you get shot at, blown up or witness what the enemy savages do to their own kind: mutilating their women, killing innocent children and having zero regard for life. Suddenly and abruptly, you no longer have the ability to look at them as human anymore. Rather, they become a disease; a viral infection that affects and kills more innocent people every single minute.

One of my most life-changing moments was the night I lost an extremely dear friend that I served with; a brother. It was just like any other night, but my team leader at the time of the operation (op), was extremely sick and was going to monitor the op over communication. So, I would fill in as acting team leader. Our fire team was not on primary entry this night, so we were going to be separated in half to cover the dynamics of the target building while the other assault force made the initial entry to the building. It was myself and Lee, our Explosive Ordnance Disposal (EOD) who was attached to our fire team, covering the front door of the target building. The other half of the fire team was covering a back alley on the adjacent side of the building. Lee was a great friend that I met when we were in selection for Team 6. It used to be that the EOD would go through the exact same selection process as the SEALs to get into the unit. Lee was our top shooter in selection and was honestly both a Navy SEAL and EOD combined with a lot of extraordinary talent, bravery and drive into one human being.

I was covering down on the front door of the target building and Lee was to my left, around the corner of the wall we were behind. The wall was approximately fifteen yards from the front door and about four feet high, which offered great cover while still leaving good observation of the target area and excellent situational awareness.

The main assault team was positioned to my right, behind the wall standing-by to move to the front door to make entry. Being that these guys were known for using explosives, we were going to do everything extremely methodically and allow the situation to develop to predict their next move. Our interpreters (Terp) yelled to the people in the house to open the doors and come out, showing their hands, so we could see that they were not armed. After a few shouts, the front door opened and a man in a white robe (man dress) was standing there looking out into the pitch black where we stood watching with about a dozen infrared lasers on his head should he make any sudden movements. The man at the door of the target building and our Terp exchanged words and he was able to get the man to come just enough outside so he would lift his man dress and show us that he had nothing concealed under his garment. Our Terp asked for all the people in the house to come outside and do the same so we could at least see that they were clean and get them away from the house to be properly searched. A couple women and children came to the entry area by the front door, but remained inside. The few of us that could see directly in the doorway could tell that there was commotion going on between the occupants of the house. This was taking too long and things between the Terp and the people of the house were turning into a confusing situation for everyone and nothing was getting done. When it appeared that this was getting more confusing by the minute, the call was made for the initial assault team to move up to the front door to get the gaggle of people back to the wall so they could start their clearance and we could search the people. The initial assault team moved up and attempted to get the people out of the house. Minutes went by with no luck! Somewhere during all this I figured that the use of Lee, our EOD, was going to be needed for searching the people and render them safe. I came over communications and suggested that he move up just outside of the front door and I would meet him there to help the initial assault team so we could free them up to get in the door. I saw Lee move up to this huge pillar that was supporting the overhang that completely covered the front porch area of the house, which was about a 45-degree angle and about seven yards away from the front door. I came up and got right next to Lee and we started going over our plan of attack to deescalate the chaos that was developing. After a few words with each other, I did a scan of the outside area and saw one too many of us in the initial assault area. It seemed like I was in mid-sentence when someone smacked me in the face and said get away...NOW! Right when I felt that, I put my left hand on Lee's right shoulder and said, "I am going to head to the back side of the wall, there are too many of us in here". He said, "No problem, I got this", and off I went, back to the gate to get behind the protected wall until the assault commenced.

I still cannot tell you what came over me, but it was something that had never happened to me before. It was as if I were being directed to get out of there with a directed quickness. I walked back to the front gate and as soon as I turned the corner and was behind the wall, there was the worst sound to ever hear...BOOM! In that moment of wrapping the corner to get behind the wall, the house that we were stacked up against blew up. I remember seeing debris fly by my head as if it were a scene from the Matrix. Only one brick made contact with me, which hit me on the back of my head. Thank God for helmets!

After I gathered my thoughts, I looked back in the courtyard to see over half the building missing and the assault team buried! There where horrific screams, dogs barking and just the sound of mass chaos filled the area of operation we were in. This was very bad! I walked up to where the front door area was and felt something grab my foot. Our military working dog that we had on target had just his head sticking out from the rubble and debris and he was now clinching down on my foot. When I noticed just how many guys were injured, I ripped my foot out from his mouth so I could start in with medically evacuating our guys. I ran over to where

Lee was and the overhang he was by was now on the ground.

Lee was underneath.

This event is not something I am proud of, because I bared quite a bit of survivor's guilt on my actions. I asked him to move up to where he became a causality, and I was right on his shoulder just seconds before the explosion went off. It took the longest time for this to go away, and still at times, it haunts me. Nonetheless, I am extremely fortunate that I moved back behind the wall when I did. If I did not, then I know for certain that I would not be here today.

A couple deployments later from the HBIED incident, I was getting ready for another deployment over to Afghanistan. I was leaving in 2-weeks and trying to finalize my divorce before I left the country. At the end of everything, I was granted custody of my 3 children. Not 50% custody, but 100% all mine and I had to provide for them all. I was in shock! I was used to being a warrior and dealing with terrorists, not playing family man, changing diapers and dealing with teenage girl issues.

This would turn out to be the greatest blessing ever, but not yet.

In the moment, I was scared, real scared! On deployment, in a combat zone, it is very simple.

There are no bills, no cell phones, no "hey can you run to the store?"

For me, it was the most peaceful place on earth. (What I just said is a problem, but that is how I felt).

Getting custody of my children started a chain reaction of shit that I did not see coming, or would even see happening. My unit was very supportive of me by keeping me around and tucking me away in a training position so I could figure out my new life as the full-time Dad and provider. As much as I loved staying at my command, it was very hard seeing my friends deploy with me being stuck back in the states. I was "daddy daycare", and I could not get passed that.

I lived on my accomplishments and suddenly I felt that all disappear with my new role in life. I thought my life was over.

Instead of talking with someone about my depression, I did what a lot of us veterans do: I started drinking. It was a daily thing. I would pick up my kids from school, go workout, then come home to make dinner. But not before pouring myself a drink and drink until it was time for bed. This was the only way I could sleep well most nights. Some nights, I would stare at the ceiling and wonder how I went through all this training only to find myself a full-time father with no help. I let my mind get the best of me, and figured I would never have a life of my own. I love my children unconditionally, but it was a huge life change for me. I never had to parent

24/7 and still manage to work. I had a newfound respect for single parents since I now was one.

As time went by, more built up issues of anger, depression, and anxiety became apparent. I would snap at my children for not really doing anything at all. I did not know how to deal with my kids. I could not ask my friends, because they were in the same place that I just came from, where everything was about us.

After indirectly asking people for guidance, I decided I would try going to church. I had never been spiritual, or ever gone to church, but it was suggested to me to try out a Christian church and see what I thought.

To be honest, I was the guy that made fun of other people going to church, thinking they were just brain washed and were not strong enough to deal with life. Yep...I was wrong again! Reluctantly, I went and felt extremely weird even walking into the facility. I felt like an imposter and an unwanted. For some reason, I could not get hooked and I needed something stronger and more in my face to catch my attention.

I was somewhat misled (thankfully) on going to a Christian boot camp event in Ada, OK. It was called Wild at Heart, which is a book by John Eldridge, put on by an Oklahoma City ministry named True North Ministries. I remember thinking that I would never go to some Christian boot camp and sing songs about how everything is awesome.

I am going to interject here and say that looking back, that that was a perfect example of what spiritual warfare is. I was in a hole and had no way to go but up, so why not give it a shot? I was going through some tough times in what felt like pretty much every aspect of my life. My drinking was out of control along with a lot of other issues; some of them being anger, anxiety and just plain old depression. My children were feeling the effects of my outbursts in anger over petty things. I felt trapped in Suckville, and I wanted out...bad! I was also still struggling being away from my teammates at my last Team and the satisfaction of deploying and the sense of pride that came with it. I felt like my adventures were over and that making it to the SEAL Teams was the pinnacle of my life; that there was no more. It was a very lost feeling and I felt alone with no end in sight.

This weekend getaway was one with no cell phones or any technology, which was a huge relief. It was a time to plug into my life and get me back to ground zero. There is not enough time to describe how amazing this experience was. I met so many amazing men who had the same issues that I had. Maybe not from the same source, but they felt the same way and the affects were the same as well. It was good to know that I was not alone and that these issues could be fixed. The best part of this whole experience is that I found Christ. Not learned about him, but found him. And, by "found him", what I really should is: I realized that he has been with me since the very beginning. The thought, or voice, I heard saying "leave now" when I was on Lee's shoulder right before the explosion that came to me was, in fact, my savior.

With this newfound love for life and Christ, and all that he has done for me, has been a new chapter in my life. I now tell my friends about all that has been healed from being saved. Some friends rejoice, while others look at me like I am crazy, but that's ok. I know what it means to be judgmental of others before I found Christ.

Currently, I am happier than I have been in a long time and have since retired after 20 years of honorable service. I founded a risk mitigation company in 2012 that I now own and operate named Contingent Group that works with a lot of high net-worth individuals and corporations in keeping their assets safe. My relationship with my children is better than it ever has been, and being a full-time dad is the greatest blessing I have ever received.

FRANK WHITTINGTON
United States Army

The year is 1970, the place is South Vietnam, in a region known as I Corp. The following is a true story based on actual events...

It was a cold rainy night in the heavy, high forest in the northern part of South Vietnam. I was but 20 years old, serving in the U.S. Army. I was assigned to Echo Company, 1st Battalion, 327th Brigade, 101st Airborne Division. I was young and proud to be assigned to an Airborne Infantry Unit, just as my dad had been during WWII. I was eager to do well, and my unit had just come from a hard-fought battle at Hamburger Hill the previous summer of 1969. We were pumped and we felt we were ready for anything after our victory at Hamburger Hill. We were invincible.

For some time, a V.C. mortar squad had been working the area in and around many locations in our area of operation. The V.C. differ from the Viet-Kong in that the V.C. are from South Vietnam and are sympathetic to the political view points of the North Vietnamese or Viet-Kong. The V.C. pose a very great challenge because they are so hard to detect. The V.C. come out to do battle and then blend back in with the rest of the citizens. About the only way to get them, is to catch them in the act or acting on information from informants – which is rare.

Two rifle squads were setting up the NDPs (night defensive positions) from Echo Company. The NDPs are established by either using natural objects like rocks, trees, depressions or by digging in using our entrenching tool, or a combination of both. Then we will usually set up a few Claymore mines in vulnerable areas and post men on watch so someone is always awake during the night. The rest of the squad will settle in and try to get some rest until it is their turn for watch.

The night was still young and I was still awake as were most all of us in my squad. About 22:00 hours, we heard a dull thud of a mortar tube go off not far from our location. We were set up about 100 yards from a mountain road and 1 or 2 miles southwest of Firebase Burmingham. We knew that none of our light infantry units carried mortars, and Firebase Burmingham was too far away for mortars to be firing that close. Our commanding officer called the command post to report, and we found out the Burmingham had mortar rounds up close. The command post gave us orders to try to get a fix on the mortars. We headed for the road and by the time we were within sight, we could see the muzzle flashes through the trees. They had their range and elevation and were firing for effect by now. We could not determine the exact location because it was too dark to triangulate. The best thing to do was to have us engage the enemy mortar squad. By the time both of our rifle squads were in position, the mortars were already done firing and they were probably tearing down; getting ready to make a hasty retreat.

We put up three illumination rounds and they were right in the middle of the road – still tearing down their mortar tubes. We caught them completely off guard. They froze just long enough for us to open fire on them. We were very excited because we knew we got lucky and happened upon the V.C. Mortar Squad.

The fire fight which ensued seemed to last forever. Both M-60 machine gunners spent nearly all their ammo. I carried an M-203, which is a combination M-16 and grenade launcher. I fired maybe 20 high explosive grenades at them. The adrenaline was really flowing and we could not stop. Finally, the small arms fire stopped and we could secure the area.

The scent of gun smoke was heavy, and the smell of blood was over-powering. We knew that this would really make us look good with the battalion commander! He had previously put out the word that he wanted the mortar squad – BAD – and whoever got them would be rewarded with some R&R. When it was all said and done, the final toll was two G.I.s dead on Firebase Burmingham due to the V.C. mortars. We got credit for stopping the terrorist mortar attacks as well as 5 enemy kills.

The battalion commander was in a very festive mood. We were all rewarded medals and a big party back at the rear area. There was food and beer for all, plus a big cake that read "Congratulations, Echo Company, 5 Kills". The party lasted into the night, and everyone celebrated except for two rifle squads.

Somehow, we could not get in the mood because the 5 kills did not make us feel victorious. You see, the famous V.C. Mortar Squad turned out to be manned by women. We killed 5 women in a hail of gun fire with hate and anger in our hearts. We just kept firing and firing with insane abandon. The most sickening thing about it, is that there were also two young girls – about 6 and 8 years old. Not a single one of us even saw them during the fire fight. The little girls were found clutching the body of one of the slain women when we rushed their position.

I will never forget the look of fear and hate as they stiffened when we pried their fingers from the woman's body.

The Army turned the girls over to the Catholic Mission in the area to possibly find their next of kin. Most of us that were assigned to the rifle squads found ourselves skipping the party and the cake. Instead, we wound up sitting on the sands of Eagle Beach, searching for some peace of mind; fearing what we had done that cold and rainy night in the mountains.

To this day, 28 years later, my heart still feels heavy with sorrow. My sleep is still interrupted with memories of their dying screams as life bled from their bodies. I still wonder if those two little girls remember my face as well as I remember theirs. What will my punishment be? Will the memories ever fade, or will my torment go on forever? Will God ever forgive these insane acts of war?

I do not have the answers to these questions. But, I do know that I must get these things out somehow before it is my turn to face God.

GAMBLE DICK
United States Marines

While I served in Vietnam, I was a very light sleeper and slept fully clothed. In the early morning darkness of November 9, 1967, I heard footsteps outside my room. By the time the light hit my eyes, I was fully awake.

"Get that damn light out of my eyes! What's going on?" "Sir, are you Lieutenant Dick?", asked the voice behind the light. "Yeah, what's up?" "The Major wants you in the TOC (Tactical Operations Center) ASAP", the voice said as it left the room. Uh oh!

I made it there in record time.

It was 4 AM and the briefing room was full of sleepy looking Marine helicopter crews. Most of them were drinking coffee and smoking cigarettes. By the time I got there the mood was subdued, the air was foul, all the chairs were taken, and the coffee urn was empty. Damn Marines! It was shaping up to be crummy day.

Everyone settled down when Major Ira Snell, the camp Commander, came through the door from the radio room. He was an imposing figure to say the least. He was big and in shape. His jaw was like a hunk of granite and the madder he got, the more he thrust it out. He was damn sure leading with his jaw this morning and he looked like a battleship churning through the North Atlantic as he strode to the front of the room.

He stepped behind a podium and gripped it with hands that looked like black bear paws. A vein popped up under the dark skin of his forehead. He was tense! He began growling at the Marines.

"Welcome to Forward Operating Base One (FOB 1) of the Studies and Observation Group, gentlemen. Our mission is to do what we are told to do, and part of that mission is to monitor the Ho Chi Minh Trail and rescue downed pilots in Laos. That's why you're here this morning. Everything you see, hear, smell, touch, or taste here, and that includes the coffee, is classified TOP SECRET. Nothing you learn here is to be shared with anyone outside this room. Does everyone understand that? Any breach of security will be dealt with quickly and severely. Everybody OK with that?" That was for the benefit of the Marines. FOB 1 was a tight knit group and word was already spreading through camp that there was trouble in Laos…again!

After a moment, Major Snell drew back a big red curtain, stamped "Top Secret" in yellow letters, which was on the wall behind the podium. It revealed a large map of our area of operations, the extreme northern portion of South Vietnam, the southern portion of North Vietnam, and the eastern portion of Laos. There were murmurs and nervous looks…and then the briefing began.

"Over the past few months, we have detected an escalation of NVA activity on the Ho Chi Min Trail in Laos. Recently we were tasked to monitor Route B-45 through what the NVA calls Base Area 611; we know it as Target Box Oscar 8. Route B-45 is a series of east-west connector trails between the main north-south corridor of the Ho Chi Minh Trail and the Ashau Valley." With that he slapped the map with the ubiquitous wooden pointer that all military briefers seemed to have. The tip rested on an area about twenty miles inside Laos. That definitely got the pilots' attention! More murmurs and nervous looks.

"Yesterday we landed two Recon Teams, call signs "Flat Foot" and "Happy Times" into this general area," he said, slapping the map with his pointer again. "Flat Foot ran into trouble almost immediately. We thought they could break contact after dark, but the NVA stayed after them. "Happy Times" was ordered remain in place and avoid contact.

Flat Foot's situation became critical. We tried to get them out last night with some Army choppers and a couple of Kingbees (H-34's from the 219th Vietnamese Air Force Helicopter Squadron). The first Army chopper got some of the team out. The second one was shot down and a Kingbee was shot down. We attempted to get the aircrews and the rest of the team out with Air Force Jolly Green Rescue Choppers. The first one made it out with some of the team but got shot up badly and crash-landed at Khe

Sanh. The second was shot down with some of the team aboard. It's a mess and you're going to help us clean it up at first light."

Major Snell turned the briefing over to the Ops Officer for further information. There wasn't much. There was heavy enemy activity in the area and he believed the NVA were using the downed aircraft and their crews as bait, hoping to shoot down more aircraft. Three helicopters had already been shot down and their crews were missing. That meant one Vietnamese crew of three, one Army crew of four and one Air Force crew of four. In addition, five of the original thirteen men on Flat Foot remained unaccounted for. Aircraft in the area continued to hear Emergency Locator Beacons, or "beepers", but did not have voice or visual contact with anyone on the ground.

The pilots went off to do pilot stuff. We Army types began organizing our mission. It was pretty straightforward. No details, no prior reconnaissance, and very little planning time. It was to be a rescue mission, which we called a "Bright Light" mission. There was no mention of the weather and we didn't think to ask.

The Americans for the mission would come from "A Team 323" on temporary duty from Okinawa. Although I was not assigned to 323, I would lead, and bear ultimate responsibility for the mission. MSG Lloyd Fisher was the Team Sergeant. Tall, quiet, and like a gunfighter of old, you instinctively knew he was the ultimate professional warrior. 2LT Rod Hoepner, the Executive Officer of 323, was junior to me so he would assist me with the responsibilities of command.

The other members of A-323 going on this mission were SGT. Ron Bock, a reluctant hero and first-class medic, SFC Gilbert Hamilton, courageous to a fault, SFC Bruce Luttrell, an energized professional, SSG Brooke Bell, a top-notch weapons man, Sp5 Ulrich Bayer, a demolitions expert, and SFC Erskine Osborne, an unlucky professional. A-323 would be augmented by MSG Charles "Skip" Minnicks, SFC Robert Cavanaugh, and SFC. Charlie Harper. "Skip" was a legendary SOG operative, and Cavanaugh and Harper were both very experienced. Minnicks and Cavanaugh were passing through our camp on their way back from a mission debrief in Saigon. They were assigned to FOB 3 in Khe Sanh but when they heard that the Hatchet Force was going out to try and find Msgt. Bruce Baxter and Specialist Joe Kusick, who remained unaccounted for, they just attached themselves to us. Charlie Harper, assigned to FOB 1, did the same. They didn't seek anyone's permission; they just got their rigs and went to the LZ west of the camp. It happened all the time when guys were in trouble.

MSG Fisher, 2LT Hoepner, and I remained to get more information, maps, radio procedures and codes. We were assigned call sign "Bull Dog" and told that our participation would last no longer than ten hours. We had to be out of the area by last light at all costs. I guessed that higher headquarters didn't want a repeat of the previous evening. "Don't take food, excessive water, or heavy weapons because you'll need to travel light and you won't be there that long," the Operations Officer said to emphasize the quick in and quick out nature of the mission.

We were to land a force of Special Forces and Cambodian mercenaries, called a Hatchet Force, several thousand meters from the site of the previous night's action. We were to work our way to the crash site(s), determine the fate of the helicopters and personnel and deal with the situation accordingly, remove any sensitive material, and get out. As usual, we were additionally tasked with taking prisoners and seizing or destroying enemy equipment and facilities. Chances of heavy contact with NVA forces were deemed to be very probable.

The Hatchet Force was ready and standing by on the helipad across from the camp entrance at 6AM. The total Hatchet Force strength for this mission was close to ninety, a huge operation by SOG standards...and an indication of just how dangerous the mission was expected to be.

Sitting in the dirt waiting for choppers and watching the sky lighten soon became tedious. The initial adrenaline surge wore off. 6 AM had come and gone; so had 7 AM. We should have lifted off an hour and a half ago but we were in the "hurry up and wait" phase for which armies around the world are so famous.

It was spring-time in the Southern Hemisphere, the dry season was ending and the monsoons were starting. This morning was hot and humid!

We eventually got a "Stand Down" order and went back into the camp to find some shade and refill canteens. I went to the TOC to get updates. The original plan was cancelled because the Marine helicopters had a previous mission. Not unexpectedly, the situation was SNAFU'd.

I went back to my room and got a can of C-Ration Peaches and stuck it in a cargo pocket of my fatigues.

We were back on the helipad about 1100 hours. The gaggle of helicopters had been rounded up and as soon as all the helicopters were topped off with fuel we would be picked up and transported to the landing zone in Laos.

Sure enough, a short while later we heard them lift off from Phu Bai Airfield just down the road. It was a short hop for them. We knew the drill and rose to meet the incoming helicopters. The Kingbees came in first and the Marine H-34's followed.

They came roaring in causing the usual commotion and stirring up the oily dirt of our landing zone. It stuck to our sweaty bodies adding to our general discomfort. No words were spoken as we stepped through the mini-cyclones created by the individual helicopters to enter the hot, noisy interiors of the H-34's. I was the last man on the first chopper so I could be the first off when we reached our LZ.

Marine gunships growled in circles above the helipad. They were a welcome sight. They didn't carry quite as much ordnance as the Army gunships, but they were very effective and well flown by courageous pilots.

Suddenly, we were away. After several hours of waiting in the hot sun, we were climbing to the cool air at 5000 feet. Flying over lush jungle and steep sided cliffs, with sunlight reflecting off the many streams and rivers under the trees. My mind wandered to more peaceful thoughts. It was beautiful country, marred by occasional bomb craters, like a beautiful girl with acne.

After about 45 minutes, the VNAF Crew Chief tugged on my sleeve and pointed to our LZ. I noticed burned areas and saw the smoke rising from the helicopter crashes and the napalm dropped by A1 Skyraiders the previous evening. Brave men had lost their lives there and no doubt a clever and determined enemy awaited us. I knew we were about to descend into a nightmare in 64 shades of green and I expected to die.

Moments later it was show time! There is no way to adequately describe the adrenaline dump that accompanies a combat air assault. It happens every time, no matter how many times you do it. And every time I've thought to myself, "If I could find a way to recreate this as a thrill ride at Disneyland it would be the ultimate E-Ticket Ride. I would be rich." There was nothing to compare it to. If real life was like the movies, this is where "Ride of the Valkyries" by Richard Wagner, or better yet, the last guitar/horn riff in "Liberation" by Chicago, would fade in as background music.

Sometimes the helicopter came screaming in at treetop level, suddenly flaring, and plopping down in a small jungle clearing, barely stopping before it powered away over the treetops. Other times it was different...but the same.

This time, we approached the LZ at a very high altitude because of concerns for enemy antiaircraft and ground fire. We were directly over the LZ when the engine went idle and the bottom fell out. We were in a death spiral toward a large grassy area on a ridgeline east of the smoke. Although we were hanging on to anything we could for dear life, there was no need; centrifugal force had us pinned inside the aircraft. There was no sound. Our fate was ruled by basic physics. We were going to die!

Suddenly the engine roared to life and we flared toward the ground. Even though I was pressed hard against the floor of the Kingbee, I managed to get my legs out the door and sit up. Whomp! We were on the ground and I was out. My exit was not elegant, but it got the job done. The eighty pounds of extra weight I carried didn't help. The Kingbee was gone, but the roaring continued as the remaining thirteen helicopters disgorged their loads and passed over me, looking like enraged dragonflies and sounding like storm driven waves crashing on the North Shore of Oahu.

It grew quiet. No helicopter noise, no voices, and no gunfire. It was time to contact the Forward Air Controller (FAC).

"Covey, this is Bull Dog, over."
"Bull Dog, Covey. Go."
"Covey, Bull Dog, the LZ is cold. We are moving out now, over."
"Roger, Bull Dog. We still have "beepers", but no voice contact, over."

The leaders of Bull Dog were finally seeing the terrain from the ground and it was problematical. We didn't have a lot of time thanks to the extremely late start we got, and would have to cross a lot of open ground to get to the crash sites before dark. Because the ground was so open along the necessary route of movement, we would split the force. I wasn't happy about doing that, but the ridge line that paralleled the main force movement and the high ground over-looking the crash sites would have to be cleared of possible enemy.

MSG Fisher started out with two members of his team and a small element of Cambodian mercenaries to secure the hilltop. Minnicks and Cavenaugh took a small force to cover the ridge.

Because time was so important, the main force moved east from the landing zone through tough, knee-high Elephant Grass. It offered no cover, concealment, or protection.

I didn't expect to make it to the crash site(s) before we made contact with NVA forces. Our only advantage was to stay on high ground as long as possible. We were thankful for the obvious presence of our FAC and the helicopter gunships. They were real deterrents to enemy attack. We were all in a hurry to find the Jolly Green crash site.

Within minutes of leaving the LZ, a blond headed Caucasian, wearing olive drab stateside fatigues, was spotted coming up a grassy draw toward the main body of the Hatchet Force. He was Sp4 Richard Jarvis, the gunner on the U.S. Army UH-1D "Huey" shot down the previous evening.

Jarvis seemed to be in pretty good shape, considering what he had been through. I asked him about the rest of the crew and the location of the downed Huey. He said everyone else was injured, and he thought Bill Whitney, the Crew Chief, was dead. Jarvis had been hiding at the bottom of the hill with Warrant Officer Bill Zanow for a while during the night, but Zanow was badly injured and not able to move much, so he sent Jarvis up the hill to get help. Jarvis thought both Zanow and Warrant Officer Kent Woolridge were picked up earlier in the day but he didn't know if they were alive. (VNAF

Kingbees picked up Zanow and Woolridge separately and transported them to Phu Bai where they both underwent emergency surgery. They also rescued the 6 souls who were aboard the Kingbee that was shot down.)

Specialist Jarvis also told me about a heavy machine gun on the other side of the valley. He was a sharp kid and gave me good information. A helicopter was called to evacuate Jarvis and Bull Dog moved on.

"Skip" Minnicks and his group found the Army "Huey" crash site. They destroyed weapons, ammunition, radios, and anything else that might be useful to the enemy. Nearby, they found the body of SSG Bill Whitney, the much beloved Crew Chief of the ill-fated "Huey". He died of wounds sometime during the night. His M-60 Machine Gun was cradled in his lap. He was the first member of the 190th Assault Helicopter Company to be killed in Vietnam.

Minnicks called for a helicopter to evacuate Whitney's body and the sad, badly flawed, process of returning him home began. His remains were delayed for over 30 days in the confusion of being an Army crewman, far from his parent unit, and sent to a Marine Corp Graves Registration facility. Once that sad task was complete, Minnicks and his group started across the face of the hill to catch up to the rest of us. The transport helicopters had returned to Phu Bai, but the Marine gunships remained over us by cycling through Khe Sanh for fuel and armament. They were a comfort. In our haste to accomplish the mission, we were getting spread out and we expected an attack.

Fisher and his group had climbed the north side of Hill 891, so named because it was 891 meters in elevation. It was muddy and almost impossibly steep. They cleared the ground that overlooked the crash areas.

The main force of Bull Dog proceeded to an area of burned "Elephant Grass" on the southeastern side of hill 891. We rejoined with Master Sergeant Lloyd Fisher just below the hilltop. There were two partially burned bodies there. They were carrying some U.S. equipment and both Fisher and I especially noted a K-Bar knife, which was issued to all U.S. Marines. There was also a pair of U.S. binoculars.

We both initially thought the bodies were Americans because of the American equipment. Lloyd read my mind when he said, "Poor Bastards." However, they were dead NVA soldiers, and they almost certainly had seen combat against our Marines.

I removed a boot from one of the dead NVA. It was canvas with a rubber sole. I had been briefed by the Intelligence officer to bring back examples of enemy footgear when possible. Just as James Bond had "Q", SOG had a group in Taiwan that provided all sorts of unique weapons and items with which we could fight, and subvert, the VC and NVA. One of their on-going projects was to equip our recon teams with footgear that would leave the same boot print as an

NVA boot, hence the need to have current examples of enemy boot treads. At one point, they even produced a boot sole that left an impression of a bare foot.

Fisher removed the U.S. binoculars. They were pretty smoked up...like looking through tinted glass, but they magnified and they might be useful. We were in a hurry to move out and I started in the direction of the Jolly Green crash site.

The terrain was deceptive and as we entered the dense vegetation in the tree line we were channeled into a deep gully. In places, it was about a yard wide at the bottom and maybe 3 yards wide at the top. There was no evidence that a helicopter had crashed there. It was the wrong ravine. And it was dangerous. I radioed the others not to follow us.

The 15 to 20 foot sides of the gully were steep and un-climbable for a large force of untrained mercenaries such as this. It would take too long to get out that way. Heavy brush grew over us, the sun was going down and it was getting dark at the bottom of the gully. The air in the gully was fetid and suffocating. It was possible that no human beings had ever walked this gully. I could understand why. We needed to get out of there.

A Soc Chan (we called him Sam), the Cambodian Battalion Commander and our lead interpreter, made his way to me looking scared and concerned.

"Sir," he said, "this is not a good place. The soldiers are very scared. We must leave this place."

I agreed and told him we were looking for a way out. I looked back at the line of Cambodian mercenaries behind me. They were Buddhists and they were very superstitious and quite intuitive. Every one of them wore an amulet on a leather thong around his neck. The amulets were little bags, usually made from a small square of red bandana, containing grains of rice and other tiny objects that had been blessed by a Buddhist Priest. When they were scared or stressed, they touched the bags in much the same way that devout Catholics fingered their Rosary Beads.

Every one of the soldiers that I could see had his "Prayer Bag" in his mouth! I had never seen them do that. Creepy! For the first time that day, I felt true fear rather than the usual dose of healthy apprehension. I quickly suppressed it and moved on.

We continued down the gully for another 30 meters and finally found a way out on the east side of the gully. Unfortunately, we wanted to go west, so we had to climb back up the hill to the beginning of the gully where we could cross to the west and help look for the crash site of Jolly Green-26. The hill was steep and slippery. With the added weight of our rucksacks, it was a tough, time-consuming, climb.

MSG Fisher found a blood trail and some U.S. bandages. His group was following the trail when one of the gunships reported seeing an American in a flight suit emerging from the tree line some distance from us. We all turned in that direction. The gunship radioed that he was almost out of fuel and might be light enough to land and pick the survivor up.

Many helicopters were underpowered. Depending on weight, altitude, heat, and humidity, they were sometimes unable to land or hover in the mountains of Laos until they had reduced their weight by burning fuel or jettisoning equipment. Pilots carefully computed what was known as the "Density Altitude Factor" when planning their flights.

The gunship crew jettisoned as much weight as they could, including rocket pods and extra machine gun ammo, and made the pick-up. We learned that the gunship had the pilot of Jolly Green-26, Captain Gerald Young, on board. The gunships left the area and those of us on the ground resumed our search for the Jolly Green 26 crash site with renewed vigor. If Captain Young survived, maybe there were other survivors!

Captain Young would later be awarded the Congressional Medal of Honor for his actions on the night of November 8/9, 1967. This entire incident would be one of the most decorated incidents of the Vietnam War for the United States Air Force.

Covey reported a new "Beeper" in a heavily wooded area about 600 meters southeast of where Captain Young was picked up. Someone in the Air Force Chain of Command wanted us to check it out. I thought that would be a particularly bad idea. We could not get to the location before it turned dark and it was in the opposite direction of the Jolly

Green crash site. I decided our best move was to keep looking for the site of the downed Jolly Green. Odds were that the "Beeper" was a trap. Someone on the radio said, "Cowards." Easy for them to say, they weren't down there.

The light was fading fast and we had not found the JG crash site. Keeping in mind that I was told to be out of the area at last light at all costs, I radioed Covey, who was still in the area. Two Marine gunships were back as well.

"Covey, Bull Dog, over."
"Bull Dog, Covey, go ahead, over."
"Covey, it'll be dark soon. I don't think we will reach the JG site before dark. We're going to find a PZ (Pick up zone), over."
"Bull Dog, Covey, stand by, over."

After several minutes, Covey called back with the news that we couldn't be picked up because a severe storm (typhoon?) had moved into the coastal areas of South Viet Nam and all the helicopters were grounded due to weather. We were advised to find a good location to RON (Remain overnight). They would come for us at first light tomorrow.

There was nothing to do but to climb back to the top of Hill 891 and prepare a night defensive position as best we could. We had few defensive armaments; no food, not much water, and many of the soldiers had nothing to protect them from the elements other than the clothes on their backs. It would be a cold night in the mountains of Laos at best. At worst, it wouldn't matter. We began our trek up the hillside in the fading light.

THUMP! A small explosion in the column behind me, and a bad situation just got worse. SFC Osborne had stepped on a "Toe Popper" (a small anti-personnel mine) and it had taken half his foot off and injured his lower leg.

Several us passed over the mine, but "Ozzie" was the unlucky one who stepped on it. I called Covey and asked for a Medevac helicopter, not really expecting to get one, but about a half hour later a Huey hovered into our hastily prepared LZ near the top of Hill 891. The sun had set and it was almost completely dark.

SGT Ron Bock, the Medic, did such a great job with SFC Osborne, that the Doctors at Phu Bai were able to save enough of his foot so that he would walk again. Ron had also been caring for a very young Cambodian who was suffering from stomach cramps. He was also evacuated on the Huey. At the last minute, another Cambodian jumped on just as the helicopter lifted off.

At first, Ron thought the guy was "bugging out", but on reflection he realized that Sam, the Cambodian Commander, had ordered him to go with and look after the sick Cambodian. Indigenous casualties were transferred to Vietnamese Hospitals for treatment. That was a real problem for our Cambodians. They were minorities and racism was alive and well in Vietnam. If the young Cambodian went into a Vietnamese facility alone, there was a good chance he might not come out, so Sam sent along a bodyguard.

In the rapidly fading light, the gunships contacted me, saying that they were almost "Bingo" fuel and would be leaving in a few minutes. I directed them to expend their ordinance on the heavy automatic weapon location described to me by Specialist Jarvis. They put rockets and machine gun fire into the dark shadows of the cliff to our south. There was no return fire. Odd!

The gunships requested that we mark our location for future reference which we did by showing strobe lights at the Eastern and Western ends of our perimeter. Unfortunately, one of the gunners on the helicopter thought the strobes were ground fire and fired about a dozen rounds at us before he was stopped. He hit one of our Cambodians, and Ron went back to work.

It was now completely dark and Lloyd Fisher and I stood atop hill 891 looking into a clear ink-black sky. The stars were appearing. At first there were hundreds, then thousands, then millions. The normally taciturn Master Sergeant Fisher stole my thoughts again when he said, "Sir, this is really bad." "Top, I'll be surprised if we see another sunrise", I replied. I sensed him nodding his head as he said, "Yep."
His reply was eloquent in its simplicity. We would fight with all our beings until we were killed. Then

it would be someone else's turn to come for us. We all silently made peace with whomever, or whatever, we believed and prepared for what lay ahead.

As instructed, Hatchet Force "Bull Dog" did not bring entrenching tools, food, or extra water, but we prepared for a night defense of Hill 891. It was difficult to dig in the clay soil with our hands but that's about all we had. We only had two machine guns and one claymore mine. This was not the Boy Scouts and we were not prepared. I should have known better.

We occupied the area just below the top of the hill. To our south the hill was relatively steep and open. A hundred meters down-slope the tree line began and covered the rest of the steep down slope. This was the area of the hill where the helicopters tried to pick up "Flat Foot". I marveled that they didn't have rotor strikes against the hillside during their night landings. It would be tricky in the daytime, but a night landing here, under heavy fire, was a feat of exceptional airmanship.

Off to the southwest, was the tree line that concealed the Jolly Green-26 crash site. Although these tree lines were dark and foreboding, they were not the greatest threat.

To our east and west, the slopes were gentler and trees extended almost to our perimeter. These were the most likely avenues of enemy approach. We placed the machine guns there and concentrated more of the force on the east and west ends of the perimeter.

To the north was the slippery cliff-like slope that MSG. Fisher and his group climbed earlier today. It is there that we set up the CP (Command Post). I respected the NVA and knew that they often used the most difficult, hence the least guarded, approach to their objective. We were vastly out-numbered and time was on the enemy's side. I wanted to be sure this approach was constantly guarded, so Lloyd and I did it ourselves. Our position also offered protection from direct fire from the other approaches, thus protecting one of the all-important radios.

Nights in the mountains of Laos got cold. Lloyd's poncho and liner had been wrapped around "Ozzie" when he was medically evacuated earlier. So, we shared mine. We were lucky to have something to keep the dew off us and to give us a little warmth. Since we believed we would be picked up in the morning, I opened the can of C-Ration Peaches and shared them with Lloyd. Everyone got ready for a long, and probably deadly, night.

"Bull Dog, Bull Dog, this is Blind Bat Zero Three, over."
After several hours of silence on the radio, this unexpected call startled me.
"Bull Dog, Bull Dog, this is Blind Bat Zero Three, over."

I respond, *"Blind Bat Zero Three, this is Bull Dog, over."*

"Bull Dog, Bat Three is inbound to your location to turn on the lights, over."

"Ahh...roger that. Say again your intention, over."

"Bull Dog, Bat Three is a flare ship. Just say the word and we will turn your night into day. It'll be so bright down there you will be able to read the fine print on your Divorce Papers, over."

We could hear the drone of the approaching C-130. Within a few minutes, we were adjusting Blind Bat-03's flare patterns and as advertised, it was as bright as day around our perimeter.

The flares came every few minutes in strings of three. We could hear the pop when the detonators ignited the flares and they sizzled and smoked like Fourth of July sparklers as they floated down under their small parachutes. They were Magnesium Flares and burned with a white-hot intensity that created very dark shadows. They swung back and forth as they came down, giving the illusion that the trees and the grass were living, animated beings. The shadows jumped back and forth and the landscape became surreal in the constantly moving bright lights. The woods were full of ghosts.

But the light was comforting and served to keep the enemy at bay. Blind Bat-03 had taken the night away.

Even more comforting was the voice on the radio. We were fully expecting an enemy attack and we believed we were in danger of being overrun. The voice high in the darkness kept us talking and helped us stay awake. Lloyd and I took turns checking the perimeter and monitoring the radio.

I could only speak for myself, but I suspected many of us on that mountainside in Laos had the same thought processes regarding the hours to come. I moved rapidly through the five stages of grief preparing myself to die.

Denial...this couldn't be happening. We should have been out of here hours ago. I was responsible for every life in our little perimeter and I took that very seriously.

Anger...this thing was really screwed up and I had no options. Other than getting Specialist Jarvis and Capt. Young off the hill alive and sending the body of a brave young American back to the land that didn't care, the day was a disaster! I had lost a good man and now another one was wounded. I felt cursed!

Bargaining...Bizarre/ I remember specifically saying to myself that if I survived and got home, I'd wash the dishes every night. I lied.

Regret...I thought of all the opportunities I'd blown. I routinely was my own worst enemy. I thought a lot about all the girls in my life who I foolishly let slip away. Each of them was wonderful and unique and deserved better treatment than they got from me. I had fond thoughts and profound regrets about all of them. These were nice thoughts and good memories to have on the eve of my impending death. But mostly, I regretted that I would probably never see my family and Linda, my unofficial fiancée (no ring yet), whom I loved more than I would ever be able to communicate.

Acceptance…I would probably die on this unnamed spot on the side of a hill in Laos; but by God, the people who killed me were going to know I was there and they would pay a heavy price for taking me out. I was at peace and I had no fear!

Once I accepted death as not just possible, but inevitable; my fear of death was banished and a sense of peace set in that made me feel very lethal and dangerous. I became much too busy to dwell on my personal thoughts and problems. There was work to be done. It would be wet and dark and dirty. We were SOG…this was what we did.

Blind Bat-03 continued to talk to us and to take away our darkness. At one point, the voice in the sky asked if we are a big force or a small force. For a moment, I was at a loss for the answer. For a SOG operation, we were extremely large, but surrounded by thousands of NVA, we felt much too small. If the NVA were listening, and they most assuredly were, I didn't want them to think that overrunning us will be easy.

I answered, *"We're a large force."*

The Bat responded, *"That's good because it looks like a Boy Scout Jamboree down there. You guys are surrounded by hundreds of camp fires."*

I answered the Bat, *"If this turns out badly, will you get word to my unit that I want my parents and my girl to know that my last thoughts were of them?"* I told him my personal call sign was "Lancer" so that he could pass the request to the right family.

The Bat promised that he would do it if necessary.

During the night, we watched a steady stream of lights climb over a low pass to the East-Southeast. In the dark, they looked like a string of pearls. Evenly spaced and never ending. Someone was counting but gave up after one hundred fifty. Judging from the movement and brightness of the lights, we thought they were trucks. A footpath showed on our map at about 4000 meters in that direction. It was undoubtedly an improved road now. The Bat didn't see them, but called for some A-1's, call sign "Pedro". "Pedro" didn't see them either and couldn't safely come down into the valley to see them from our perspective because of the terrain, so the NVA got a pass and would live to die elsewhere someday.

The NVA were very proficient with their road building and camouflage. They used trellises to train and secure the second and third canopies of foliage over their roads and trails making the paths invisible from the air. It was obvious to us that they had expanded the footpath into a roadway and cleverly camouflaged it from aerial observation. The lights continued to move even with the aircraft overhead and the flares to their west. The lights continued all night long.

After several hours, Lloyd and I agreed that maybe we should turn out the lights. Although we were surprised that we had not been attacked yet, we wanted to be sure that if an attack occurred, there would be enough flares to light the battlefield.

Lloyd passed that decision to the Bat and the Bat responded, *"We were going to suggest that. We're going to go west a little bit to check something out, but if you need us we'll only be a few minutes away."*

The drone of the C-130 faded off to the west and we were alone in the dark. Our night vision began to return. All remained quiet.

A short while later the Bat was back and informed us that there were heavy anti-aircraft guns to the southwest being moved in our direction. The area was a little hot for them so they would orbit in our area until their replacement flare ship arrived.

"Bull Dog, Bat Zero Three, over."

"This is Bull Dog, go ahead."

"Bat Three, we're about ready to RTB (Return to Base). "Lamplighter" will take over from us. We have briefed him and he should be on station in a few minutes. Good luck, Bull Dog...you may need it. And don't worry, I'll check back and if I need to relay your message, I will. Blind Bat, out."

"Bull Dog, Bull Dog, this is Lamplighter, Lamplighter, over."

"Lamplighter, Bull Dog, go ahead"

"Bull Dog, we're in the area and we want to kick out a flare for you to adjust, over."

"Roger, Lamplighter. Go ahead."

We didn't hear a plane and we didn't see a flare. We reported this to Lamplighter.

"Roger, Bull Dog. We'll drop another flare."

Nothing.

This went on for about fifteen minutes and Lamplighter was getting more and more agitated. We lit up a strobe light, but Lamplighter saw nothing. Finally, I asked, *"Lamplighter, Bull Dog. Do you see a lot of campfires?"*

The answer was negative.

The C-130 widened its orbit and eventually we heard the drone of its engines and vectored it into our general area. They had been looking for us many miles away. Lloyd requested that Lamplighter hold the flares. If we were hit with a ground attack, Lamplighter would know by the tracers. If they saw tracers, turn on the lights.

The calming rapport that we had with Blind Bat was gone. The radio remained silent except for a call from the nighttime Airborne Battle Command and Control Center (ABCCC), a C-130 using the call sign, "Alley Cat" requesting a SitRep (Situation Report) and "Iron Spud", an Army Mohawk Surveillance Aircraft from the 131st Aviation Company in Phu Bai checking to see if we had radio traffic for FOB 1. "Alley Cat", and "Iron Spud" would always check on teams in the field at night. It was comforting to know that someone would eventually establish contact during the dark, lonely nights in Laos. If nothing else, it would help establish a time of death.

I told both aircraft that our situation was static. Although we were surrounded, we had not been attacked.

Then, the one thing that we thought would not happen, did. It was almost imperceptible at first. The sky in the east began to lighten. It was a dangerous time on the battlefield. The enemy frequently attacked during the hours just before dawn because defender's senses were dulled and their alertness waned. The American team members brought the perimeter to full alert and prepared for an attack that never came.

We made it through the night! Now all we had to do was finish the mission by finding and processing the Jolly Green 26 crash site. Then we could be picked up and flown back to Phu Bai for the traditional breakfast of steak and eggs that the Mess Sergeant always prepared for returning teams.

A delicious thought that obviously wasn't going to pan out. As the sky in the east became lighter, we saw the huge banks of clouds. Helicopters would be unable to reach us today. We were at the mercy of the enemy and the elements. It was time to worry about the things we could control, not the things we couldn't.

Breakfast wasn't an issue. We had no food. Most of us had not eaten since dinner two nights ago. Our water supply was low, but we didn't think thirst would be a problem. In a few hours, we would probably have more water than we needed. The clouds were blowing toward us. There was already a high overcast above us.

We would split the force. One group, with some of the Senior NCO's and LT Hoepner, would find the Jolly Green crash site. I would keep a force to secure the top of the hill and act as radio relay and reinforcement if the troops at the crash site ran into trouble.

It was time to go to work.

The clouds were moving in quickly and the ceiling was lowering. Not only would we be stuck here, but we also wouldn't be getting any air support or resupply for a while due to the worsening weather. A light drizzle started just after the group going in search of the Jolly Green 26 crash site disappeared into the tree line a hundred meters or so to our southwest.

Those of us manning the hilltop consolidated our perimeter and put out Observation Posts to our east and west. The mountaintop to our south was now shrouded in clouds. The drizzle softened the clay soil somewhat and we were able to dig a little deeper. Unfortunately, water also collected in the bottom of the holes and would make the coming night just a little more miserable. Our situation could only be worse if we were under attack. I kept wondering why we weren't? What were they waiting for; they had all the advantages and we were so vulnerable. Our force was split, the weather was bad, and they out-numbered us by thousands.

In my opinion, there were several factors working in our favor:

Our force was larger than the usual rescue force and the NVA were not initially prepared to deal with us. They were set up around the crash site prepared to shoot down more rescue helicopters and supporting aircraft or to ambush a small rescue team. Our large insertion caught them unprepared.

Just as the weather and terrain were making things difficult for us, it slowed down the enemy as well. It could take the NVA several days to bring in and position a force large enough to take us out in a quick, decisive engagement. They would want to avoid a protracted battle because, if the weather cleared and we regained our air support, the cost to them might be more than they were willing to bear. However, if the weather stayed bad for several days, it would negate our air power advantage and improve the odds of their success.

Finally, and probably most important, the enemy troops in the area seemed to be on a mission and could not afford the time or resources to deal with us. They were listening to our radio transmissions and knew that our mission was to rescue and recover. They guessed that we would try to avoid enemy contact. They were satisfied with containing us and continuing their mission. They took what they could get without suffering too many losses. If we made a serious mistake, they would exploit it, otherwise, let sleeping dogs lie.

The Rescue/Recovery element reached the JG-26 crash site. Almost immediately SFC Bruce Luttrell found the Flight Deck of JG-26. He could make out two bodies, imbedded in the wreckage. Identification couldn't be positively made in the field, but Dog Tags on the remains indicated that the two were Captain Ralph Brower, the co-pilot of JG-26 and Staff Sergeant Eugene Clay, the Flight Engineer.

While the team Medic, Ron Bock, began the grisly and painstaking task of removing the remains of two U.S. Air Force men from the wreckage of the big Sikorsky CH-3 Jolly Green Giant helicopter, other members of the team fanned out in search of other victims or survivors. Once removed, the remains of the two Air Force men, with the Dog Tags affixed to them, were moved to the center of the small perimeter set up by the team and gently laid upon a poncho.

The main cabin area of JG-26 was near-by. There was another body in this portion of what was left of the helicopter. Ron believed this was the body of Sp4 Joe Kusick because of the radio parts and antenna from the PRC-25 Radio on the body. The body did not have Dog Tags. SOG Teams never wore Dog Tags in Laos. Ron, with the help of Brooke Bell, extricated Joe's remains and added them to the poncho containing the remains of the two Air Force men in the center of the perimeter.

All this work was being accomplished in misty rain and intermittent showers.

The ground party at the crash site saw two individuals watching them from the ridgeline. Thinking that they might be survivors, a squad started toward them; but their actions were suspicious and it was quickly determined that they were enemy soldiers. Perhaps they were trying to lure our troops into an ambush...a typical NVA tactic. The squad returned to the crash site and the two enemy soldiers disappeared. It left no doubt that there were NVA about and they were monitoring our activities.

Charlie Harper and Lloyd found another Air Force crewman's body at the bottom of a ravine in a fairly flat and open area. It had to have been SGT Masey, the para-rescueman from Jolly Green 26. They also found a body towards the top of the same ravine. Both bodies were downhill from the wreckage. When JG-26 was shot down, Covey 57 reported seeing one person, on fire, running downhill from the crashed JG-26.

Ron and Rick Bayer joined Charlie Harper at the body at the top of the ravine. It was 38 meters downhill from the crash site, badly burned and entangled in jungle growth in a narrow ravine cut into a very steep part of the hill below the wreckage of JG-26. The body was lying face up and it was definitely MSG Bruce Baxter, the team leader of Flat Foot. Although all his clothing had burned off, his face was recognizable.

Extrication of the bodies would be extremely difficult due to the weather, terrain, enemy activity, and condition of the bodies. They decided it would be best to lift the remains straight up with a helicopter rather than try to drag them out of the gully and up the hill. Rick Bayer and Ron Bock rigged the bodies for extraction using some rappelling rope.

We believed that all souls were accounted for and that seemed to be the consensus at all levels of command. Although the Air Force had terminated its search and rescue activity, they were keeping helicopters on standby to come for the remains if the weather broke. It was raining harder. The decision was finally made to stand down because the forecasters said the weather wouldn't break before nightfall.

The Rescue/Recovery element began the climb up the steep, wet hillside to our perimeter at the crown of Hill 891. All remains that were recovered were left at the crash site for helicopter recovery when the weather cleared. Moving the remains up the hill would have been extremely difficult and probably would have taken several hours, even though the distance was only 300 yards or so. Weather, terrain, and the enemy conspired against us.

We all took a break and dined on no-cal meals of nothing and then set about consolidating and refining the perimeter for the coming night defense. It was raining lightly, but steadily, so we made sure everyone filled their canteens.

A short time later, several of the mercenaries began talking excitedly and pointing downhill. SFC Hamilton was the first American to see them . . . a platoon of NVA (maybe 30 or more) walking single file from west to east along a trail at the bottom of the hill. He took the binoculars that were taken from the NVA body the day before and tried to get a better look.

"Look at that! There's a Caucasian leading them. He has a white Pith Helmet and a red beard"

I could see the Pith Helmet without using the binoculars. Several recon teams had reported seeing a red bearded Caucasian, perhaps a Russian Advisor, wearing a Pith Helmet. I thought he was a myth, but maybe he was real.

Lloyd checked it out with the binoculars and agreed that he might be a Caucasian. Lloyd plotted the NVA position on the map. The NVA were at least 1000 meters downhill from us. Gilbert Hamilton set the bi-pod of an M-60 Machine Gun on a stump in the middle of our perimeter. I looked through the binoculars and told Gilbert that it was an impossible shot. It was beyond effective maximum range and downhill. He responded in his usual fashion, "Bull shit!"

He opened up with the M-60 as I watched through the binoculars. I was skeptical but ready to adjust his fire. I was amazed to see NVA falling, including the guy we thought was the Russian. I looked over at Gilbert and he had the M-60 pointing at the sky, launching bullets like the Machine Gun was a Mortar. This guy was Davy Crockett, Alvin York, and Houdini all in one. What shooting . . . and in the rain to boot!

On the other side of the perimeter, SSG Bell was doing the same with the other M-60. SFC Cavanaugh was bent over hands on knees and Bell had mounted his machine gun on Cavanaugh's back so he could get enough elevation to engage the NVA. He was cheering as he shot. I was in awe.

I looked back at the NVA and some of them were running for the tree line, others were dragging dead and wounded, and some just stared at the top of the hill. I could only imagine what must be going through the minds of the NVA under attack. Bullets were falling on them from the thick clouds like lead raindrops. It took them many seconds to identify the source of the incoming Machine Gun rounds. The superstitious nature of their culture caused them to panic.

The NVA disappeared into the tree line.

SFC Hamilton had a little grin on his face. Only one in a thousand marksmen could make that shot. He and Brooke had exacted some revenge for the men wrapped in a poncho a few hundred yards below us waiting for a ride home that sadly would never come.

I radioed Covey to get a "Sky Spot". There was no way that fighter-bombers could come through the clouds to deliver air-strikes in this weather but we might be able to get bombs on the suspected enemy position by using a radar-bombing technique. Lloyd had the coordinates ready.

It was a time-consuming process, so we made the request a "Prairie Fire Emergency" to speed things up. They were powerfully magic words, not to be used indiscriminately. Our request moved up to THE first priority for air support. Within fifteen minutes Covey radioed, *"Bull Dog, get your heads down. You'll have bombs in thirty seconds!"* We complied. Normally "Sky Spots" were not authorized within 2000 meters of friendly personnel . . . and that's when the winds were much more predictable. However, the magic words "Prairie Fire Emergency" had over-ridden normal policies and the bombs were released to strike a point about 1200 meters from us.

In about twenty seconds we heard a sound like a freight train coming and the bombs came whooshing out of the clouds to land right on the target. There was a huge secondary explosion and a large box-like object trailing smoke and fire came up from the trees and traveled about 400 meters east before landing and exploding in the jungle.

Faint sounds of the "spooked" and wounded drifted up to us from the bombed location. First, they were hit by lead rain and then an aircraft they neither heard nor saw had bombed them. They were panicked! And I feared we may have poked a hornet's nest with our stick.

The bombing results were radioed to Covey and we got back to work on our perimeter. Covey advised he would have to RTB but would be back before sundown to check on us.

A short while later SGT Bock detected movement in the trees to the west. He engaged, killing at least one NVA. When he fired, the Cambodians started firing! They didn't need much excuse to fire their weapons. Fortunately, we got them to cease-fire in just a few seconds. We might need all the ammo we could get later. The little firepower demonstration had served to let our enemies know that we packed a punch and that we wouldn't be an easy victory for them.

It became quiet for a while and we used the time to strengthen our perimeter. The NCO's and I were walking around the perimeter checking things out. I left the radio propped against the same stump that SFC Hamilton used to elevate his Machine Gun a few hours ago. I looked over and saw him talking on the radio and I started in his direction. As I got closer, I over heard him say, "Fuck you, bitch!"

What now? "Who are you talking to?" "Some Russian bitch. She wants us to surrender."

Several days ago, one of the teams had reported hearing Russian being spoken on the radio. Although Intelligence at the highest levels steadfastly maintained that there were no Russian advisors in the field, more than a few of SOG's Recon Teams reported seeing or hearing Russian or Chinese members with NVA units.

As impressed as I was by SFC Hamilton's usual eloquence, I was even more impressed by what he had just said. "What? Give me that handset." I demanded. "This is Bull Dog six. Who is this, over?"

A female voice speaking excellent, but accented, English responded, "This is Lieutenant Colonel Ludmila something or other, Advisor to the People's Army of Vietnam."

I knew I should terminate the conversation immediately and switch to an alternate frequency, but I couldn't. It was just too unreal. I knew that the enemy was using direction-finding equipment to try and triangulate the source of my transmissions, but I was compelled to listen and respond for a few more seconds.

Lyudmila something or other continued, something to the effect that, "You are brave men and honorable warriors and there is no need for you to die. If you come to the bottom of the hill and surrender, you will not be harmed and will be treated with respect."

I couldn't help myself. Taking a page from SFC Hamilton's Book of Radio Procedures, I replied, "Fuck you, bitch. You come up here and surrender to us." Then I switched the radio to the alternate frequency and listened for a few moments to make sure the Russian wasn't on the alternate frequency as well. It seemed clear.

SFC Hamilton said, "See, I told you."

Apparently, no one else overheard us and no record of the Russian transmission exists today. SFC Hamilton died less than three months later of wounds received on January 17, 1968, when we were on another rescue/recovery mission. It is my word against the world regarding this conversation . . . but it happened.

I stayed there with the handset cradled on my shoulder so I wouldn't miss any attempt to contact us. It was obvious to me that something big was going on and that the NVA troops in the area were much better equipped and advised than what we had been used to. There was no one to relay this information to and no way to know if the transmission was monitored by any intelligence gathering unit.

Sometime later, we all heard the unmistakable sound of a mortar round leaving the tube somewhere to the west or southwest. We all dove for cover. Ron Bock threw his body over the Cambodian soldier who was wounded last night to protect him from the incoming mortar round. About ten seconds later there was a "Crump" outside our perimeter to the northeast. The shot was long. A gray cloud of dust and smoke drifted westward from the explosion.

"Foop" another round was on the way. "Crump", still northeast, but closer. "Foop", "Crump" five more times. The rounds were close, but the NVA didn't have our range. Then it stopped. They had probably expended all the rounds they had carried up the hill.

About an hour later, Covey was back. A panicked voice on the radio was saying:

> "Bull Dog, Bull Dog, this is Covey, over." Before I
> could answer, it came again.
> "Bull Dog, Bull Dog, this is Covey, Covey, on alternate,
> over."
> I answered, "Covey, Bull Dog, go ahead."
> "We've been calling and calling and finally switched to
> the alternate. What happened to you?"

I replied with the information about Lyudmila something or other and was met with the expected skepticism. I told them that other than a brief and ineffective mortar attack, things were relatively quiet. I advised that we would need another alternate frequency in case this one got compromised. I was told, *"Stand by."*

I could hear him relaying the information and request back to the Radio Room at Phu Bai. I could only hear Covey's side of the conversation, but it was easy to tell that there was skepticism and concern in the Radio Room at Phu Bai.

Covey got back to me with a new encoded alternate frequency and the information that the weather in our area should begin to break after dark. We were to be ready for extraction early tomorrow morning. I informed him about the bodies by the wreckage of JG-26 and our plan to winch them out by helicopter.

We again dined on nothing, although some of the Cambodians had found some grubs in a couple of the old logs near the perimeter and were happily eating away. It was getting dark and we were getting ready for another long night. After the brief combat encounters this afternoon, we fully expected to receive a visit from the guys down the hill sometime during the coming night.

Bruce Luttrell slid into our hole and said, "Here sir, take this." I asked, "What is it?" and he said, "It's a "Green Hornet". It'll help you stay awake." I took it.

As the last rays of the sun began to fade we thought we could see small patches of clear sky to the east.

One more night and we could really think about getting off this hill. Lloyd and I discussed Pickup Zone options and how to evacuate the remains. We would have to go back to the east for a good PZ, but first we must go to the ravine leading down from the crash site to hook up the remains to a winch cable from one of the helicopters that would have to hover over the crash site. We could send a detail, with security, down first thing in the morning. It shouldn't take more than fifteen minutes to remove the remains once the "choppers" got there.

We got settled in and once again Lloyd and I took turns monitoring the radio and checking the perimeter. It was going to be a long night and I didn't think the "Green Hornet" was helping. I was really "on the nod".

The weather was clearing nicely and the clouds above us were shredding and thinning. It wasn't long before we were in the clear. "Blind Bat" checked in to tell us he was in the area and could be over us in minutes if we needed light. We advised the Bat that we would not call for flares unless we were in contact with the enemy, but we appreciated his presence and help. The drone of his far-off engines served notice to the enemy that we were not alone and had help standing by.

A short time later "Alley Cat" came up on the radio. I could tell from the voice that it was probably the Airborne Battlefield Commander himself who was talking. He advised that they were lining up plenty of assets (fighter-bombers) for the morning and that they would be getting us out at first light and for us not to worry. If we needed anything tonight he would personally see to it.

The night passed peacefully with only an occasional radio call. We were all grateful and surprised that we had not been in large-scale combat on this hillside. The greatest battle of the night for me was staying awake. The "Green Hornet" was highly over-rated in my opinion.

The sun was rising and so were we. Tired, hungry, muddy, and cold, we waited for the first radio contact of the morning so we could relay our plans and get everything going. Lloyd put together a detail to return to the crash site and hook up the remains. They started down the hill just before Covey arrived overhead.

Covey checked in and advised that the extraction force was airborne and should reach our location in about twenty minutes. I replied, "*Negative. We need one H-34 with a hoist, a chase ship, and some gunship escorts to precede the lift ships by about thirty minutes. We need to lift out the remains.*"

Covey replied, "*Negative on that. They want you out now! They do not want any helicopters hovering in this area. Orders are to move to a Pick Up for extraction, over.*"

I reiterated our concerns only to be told more forcefully that I would move the troops to a PZ post haste! I had no option but to call Lloyd and his group back. I wasn't leaving any living friendlies on this hill if I could help it. Covey then offered some A-1's for air strikes on any targets I had.

I advised Covey where our PZ was and he directed a pair of A-1's with rockets, napalm, and cannons onto the tree line overlooking the PZ. I had Covey put the second pair of A-1's on the tree line where Ron shot the NVA soldier yesterday. I was on the west side of the perimeter with Ron.

I put out a day-glow orange panel and requested the strike about 50 meters to the west of the panel. That's "danger close" for an air strike, but I had unshakable confidence and affection for the big, single engine, prop planes and the men who flew them. From an Infantryman's perspective, the A-1's, variously known to us as "Spads", "Hobos", or "Sandys", were undeniably the finest fixed wing close air support aircraft in the history of the world. It didn't hurt to have some of the most dedicated and courageous pilots in the Air Force holding the sticks either.

I had to violate one of the first rules of close air support. Never direct the aircraft directly over your position, but the terrain dictated how it would have to be done. The first Hobo came in from the east, directly over the perimeter at about one hundred feet and released two silver canisters of napalm. His release point seemed well to our east and the cans of napalm tumbled lazily in his wake as he roared over our heads. The "napes" caught glints of morning sun making them sparkle a bit as they tumbled toward us in slow motion. This was going to be close, I thought. But it wasn't. The napalm hit the mark and sprayed its burning contents into the tree line. There was a "Whoosh", the crackling of wood burning...and the enemy. Another pass by the wingman and we were ready to move out.

We started toward the grassy area to our east. Lloyd caught up and he was not happy. "We didn't finish the mission," he said.

"I know. I didn't have any choice. The birds were already inbound when they made the first radio call. They don't want to hover a helicopter down there and I can't say as I blame them. They just want us out as soon as possible."

Ron put the wounded Cambodian on the first chopper. I got on the last "Chopper" out, a Kingbee. We took a few hits but it was anti-climactic. Everyone got back to Phu Bai in one piece. We had our steak and eggs. We were ravenous and some of us had two or three helpings. A quick debrief and we were told to "Hit the sack". Then the "Green Hornet" kicked in and I was wide awake for the next eighteen hours. The next morning, I was off to Saigon for a debriefing at MACV Headquarters.

The debriefing in Saigon was scheduled to last a week. The actual debriefing only took about four hours...just long enough for me to be called a liar.

Apparently, there were no Russian Advisors anywhere near Laos, there couldn't be a trail or road where we saw the lights, and I was just a scared young Lieutenant trying to pass myself off as some kind of hero. That seemed to be the standard operating procedure for SOG teams. Bring in hard won information and have it disregarded. Despite the guys that were dying trying to get critical information for the chain of command, the higher ups seemed to put more credence in what Jane Fonda had to say.

The remainder of the week was intended for time to unwind; but wallowing in one of the great "fleshpots" of Southeast Asia was not my "thing". I was back in Phu Bai a day later. I didn't feel much like being among strangers. I failed the mission.

On July 4th, 2005, I attended the unveiling of a Veteran's Memorial in Chester, New Jersey, dedicated to Larry Maysey, the Para-rescueman on JG-26. It was a beautiful ceremony. My friend, Rick Fuentes, the Superintendent of the New Jersey State Police provided the State Police Pipe Band for the ceremony. "Amazing Grace", as played on the pipes, is something to be remembered. It should only be played in the presence of Warriors in my opinion.

Rick and several other New Jersey State Troopers and their families met my wife and me for lunch after the official ceremony. I appreciated it more than I could express. I told Larry Maysey's Aunt and

Uncle what I knew and assured them that Larry didn't suffer on the side of that hill and that he died with honor and courage. I believe that. It was an emotional day!

For over forty-five years I've lived with the thought that I should have done more to get the remains out. The families of those men we left on the hill deserved closure. I don't know what else to do now but help write the story so that maybe some of the people who spit at my uniform when I got back will realize that a great many of the men and women who went to Vietnam were courageous and dedicated, to each other, as well as the United States of America. And those who made the ultimate sacrifice deserve respect regardless of one's personal feelings about that time and place.

Lloyd and Ron went back in 2003 with members of the Army's Central Identification Laboratory to finish the job for which we were sent to Hill 891, but there was nothing left in the area.

Not long ago I voiced my feelings of failure to Paul Gregoire, one of the Marine pilots who took us in and came back for us later and he responded, "Bullshit! You guys should've been wiped out and you weren't. We brought out more people than we took in and that's a success in my book!"

I guess I'll have to live with that.

GARY BROWN
United States Army

In 1992, civil engineers were needed for the build-up of Ali Al Salem, Air Base, Kuwait. This was after Desert Storm, where the United States kicked Sadaam's forces out of the country and back to Iraq. This campaign was called "Operation Southern Watch". The Army was listening and watching Sadaam break the rules, which he agreed to, of the no-fly zone almost every day.

We would travel on a military rotator. This is a very large Aircraft, contracted to transport troops to and from the A.O.R., (Area of Operation). On the way over, we stopped at Frankfort Germany to refuel and change crews. Then we stopped in Shannon, Ireland, Oman, and finally arrived at Kuwait International Airport.

As we were walking across the ramp to the holding area, I noticed a c-130 cargo plane sitting near a hanger. It had plywood walls all around it. I had been around a lot of aircraft over the years and thought this was very unusual. I later found out the plane was trying to land there in a dust storm and hit the ground so hard it forced the landing gear up inside the aircraft, killing 3 Air Force Reserve members from Texas.

We went inside to a holding area and were given instructions about travel to the base where we would wait until the buses arrived. It was very hot and dusty. We had lunch, a bottle of water and an M.R.E. Then, a bathroom break in a port-a-potty. If you have never used a port-a-potty that has been sitting out in the 130-degree heat for a few days, well, it's not a good experience. But, it is better than a straddle trench, which I've had to use in field conditions.

After about an hour, the buses arrived. We were told to leave the curtains closed and to not look out; someone might take a shot at you. We were escorted by Special Forces that were driving black S.U.V.s with blacked-out windows. They would block all intersections ahead of us and we would never slow down. We made a very fast trip to the Air Base; it was about 40 miles.

The base, Ali Ah Saleam, was built on top of a hill overlooking the runway. The Patriot missile batteries were there. The Army uses them to shoot down the enemy's missiles if they fired them toward us. Also, the French were there with the French Mirage. This is their fighter aircraft. They were also flying reconnaissance missions.

We arrived at the basketball courts. We unloaded our gear and were told to walk over to the dining facilities. This was the largest building on the base and we would get our in-country briefing there.

We went inside and, thankfully, it was air-conditioned. This was great because it was about 130 degrees outside. The first sergeant came in, welcomed us to the rock, and began to tell us the significance of the base. He gave us the do's and don'ts about going into town - Kuwait City.

I later found out why they nicknamed the base the rock. The ground is rock everywhere and very hard to dig in.

A few minutes later, some guy came in screaming something in Arabic and waving an AK-47 over his head.

He was dressed in Arabic clothes and had the rag on his head; hence Ragheads. He definitely had our attention.

I thought, "It's over! The enemy has overrun the gate guards and broken through. We are all going to die." Then he stopped, laid down his weapon and took off his head rag. He had a beard and looked like a terrorist. He said he was with the Special Forces operation team and they were working with the local towns and villages to find the bad guys.

I thought, that just took ten years off my life. I could have done without that, but it was pretty good stuff. It showed me just what some of our soldiers can do and it was very impressive. They told us there were designated areas to walk that were marked with caution tape. If you got off the path, you might step on an anti-personnel mine. There were also U.X.Os, (unexploded ordinance) in the area. There were areas that had not been cleared by the engineers. That was why we got the imminent danger pay: an extra $150.00 dollars a month for risking our lives.

Then it was off to tent city, which would be our home while we were there. It was a small base and there were not many vehicles. We walked most of the time, unless we were driving a piece of equipment. There were several jobs we needed to complete.

The government would rotate guard and reserve units in and out working on these projects all over the world to provide training and to save the department of defense money.

Our first job was to complete the concrete floor for the G.P.S. (general purpose shelter), that was to be put on it. The shelter was down on the flight line about a half mile away. We would work mostly at night, taking the shelter down and hauling it a piece at a time up to the site.

We were told before the deployment to watch out for the scorpions and the camel spiders, that they were everywhere. I thought that was just a story and I probably would never see them. That was wrong; they really were everywhere. As we were taking the building down, we found several scorpions and the camel spiders were running all around, too.

Most of the work was accomplished at night because it was around 130 degrees during the day. We finished the concrete and put the building up. Our new building would be used for the Base Theater and a welcoming center. When it was finished, it had lights, carpet and air conditioning. It was one of the nicest buildings on the base.

One day, I was grading roads and happened to hook the sewer line with the grader blade. The line happened to be the main line from the latrines to the cesspool. I learned an important lesson that day about being careful. Most of the lines were only an inch underground because the ground was so hard.

I came in from work one day and was walking by the smoking pit next to the bunker when I noticed the usual people there and one of the ladies was upset. I later found out that a 22-year-old security police troop had come in from mission patrolling the perimeter. He went to his bunk and never woke up. They found him dead.

The story was that the temperature in the Hummer they were driving on patrol could reach one hundred sixty degrees. That's too hot for anyone. The daily temp on a clear day could reach over 130 degrees, and if there was a sand storm, the temp would drop to around 115.

After that, we were a lot more careful about the heat and always took plenty of water breaks. No one would ever get on to you for taking a break. We made it a point to drink at least a gallon of water a day. We did not drink anything but juice for breakfast.

One evening at the smoke pit, I was talking to an airman from Texas. I told him I was from Oklahoma. He said he had a brother that worked in Oklahoma City at the Caterpillar shop. His brother happened to be the guy that picked up our hydraulic parts for repair, at the electric company where I worked as a civilian. I was good friends with him.

That was the way it was. It was not unusual to run into someone from home on a deployment. No matter where we went, it seemed like home was not far away. One evening after work, the boss and I went to the tank graveyard. It was about 5 miles from the Rock. We passed through a check point with Kuwaiti military guards and proceeded out to the site to take pictures. This place was unbelievable. There were blown up tanks, at least 20 acres of them. Another 20 to 30 acres of buses, 20 to 30 acres of artillery pieces, and trucks.

The story was, that after the U.S. stopped Sadaam Husain in Kuwait City, he was told his troops would walk back to Iraq. They did not, of course. They started driving their equipment. The U.S. Navy and Air Force stopped them.

That highway they were on is called the highway of death.

There were hundreds of pieces of equipment including tanks, artillery pieces, buses and trucks that were destroyed, along with several hundred Iraqis.

One weekend, the N.C.O.I.C., a Master Sergeant from Andrews Air Force Base, D.C., planned a trip into Kuwait City. There was not a cloud in the sky and it seemed you could see for miles.

As we left the base, we saw an aircraft that was not far from the road. It looked like it was in a junk pile along with old trucks, cars and trash. Something you would never see around our bases back home. The road was fairly new and marked well. I was impressed because that was the business I was in; building roads and grounds maintenance.

It was about 40 miles to the city. I was shocked because a lot of the cars we saw were Chevy Impalas. The Kuwaiti's love their American cars. We stopped and parked near some shops. There were a lot of Arabs there with their traditional Arab dress, but there were foreigners there also.

I learned the Kuwaiti's do not work; they share in the wealth of the country. According to where they are on the family tree, they get their paycheck monthly. All the work that is done is done by people from India, Pakistan, Bangladesh, Sri Lanka, and the Philippines.

After buying some blankets, we went back to the truck. As we approached the truck, the Master Sergeant said, "Let's check for bombs under the truck". There are people here that don't want us here, and they could have been trying to kill us.

We drove to downtown Kuwait City, right on the coast. You could see the super tankers lined up, one after another, waiting to fill up with oil. It was an awesome sight. There were lots of tall buildings and everything was impressive. You could tell there was a lot of money there.

We parked in a square with buildings all around. There were a lot of gold shops, jewelry, music, and banks. It seemed like there was a bank on every corner. It was noon and time to get something to eat. We found a little shop not far from the parking lot. A guy was selling some kind of beef on a rotisserie heated by an infrared heater. There were tables and chairs on the sidewalk in front of the shop.

The sergeant said to order a Swrama. It was kind of like a torte with goat meat, some pickled carrots and hot peppers. We were sitting in the sun, 130 plus degrees, eating hot Sormas with sweat dripping off our faces. We were laughing at the time we were having.

It seemed like a crowd was building around us, which made us feel uncomfortable, so it was time to leave. I think they were as curious about us as we were them, but we were not taking any chances.

We walked around and bought some things then headed back to the base. On the way back, we saw a guy, an Arab, riding a camel along the road. There was not much to look at but sand. Just sand and more sand. I was sure we would die if the vehicle broke down. You could not survive in this country. It was over 130 degrees every day and if you had to walk a few miles without water, you would surely die. We were 20 miles from the City and 20 miles from the Base, out in the middle of nowhere. I was in no way going on any more trips. You could not drag me off that Base. We did make it back to the Base that night and what a relief.

One morning, I went over to start a dump truck that I had loaned to the Army so they could haul sand to fill sand bags. The fuel shut-off switch had come loose and the truck would continue running. So, I thought I would fix it rather than turn it into the motor pool because if I did, I would not get it back and we had too much work to get done.

I squeezed in between the front tire and the fender with wrenches and adjusted the switch. I was coming out when I hit my chin on the tire and bit my tongue. I jerked my head back, not aware of the sharp screw above my head. I felt the screw tear my scalp and I felt something warm running down my face. Then, the lights went out. When I woke up, there were four soldiers with first aid kits working on me. They took me to emergency medical. I walked in and there were soldiers with bug bites and one guy had a large piece of lumber stuck through his hand. I was treated and released.

The night we were to leave, we staged our equipment on the basketball court near the road where the buses and trucks would soon arrive to take tools and equipment to the airport. The camel spiders were everywhere, running around and people would step on them. I spent three weeks there and that was enough.

On the way home, we stopped in Cairo, Egypt to refuel. As we approached the airport, we could see the Pyramids. We were not allowed to leave the aircraft for the refueling, which was very unusual. It was well over one hundred degrees on the plane and very uncomfortable. I was ready to get home.

I had a lot of good times in the Reserve and was around a lot of good senior NCO (Non-Commissioned Officers), that helped me to grow up.

It was never my intention to travel the world, although I have traveled a lot. I have seen Germany, East Germany, the Brandon Burg gate, Hitler's Nazi S.S. headquarters museum, Belgium, France, Holland, Lichtenstein, Luxemburg where General Patton is buried, Ireland, Cypress, Egypt, Saudi Arabia, Oman, Bahrain, Cyprus, Qatar, Kuwait, Iraq, Turkey. Central American countries of Panama, Honduras, El Salvador, Nicaragua, and Mexico. I have been to most of the United States and

Canada. Out of all those places, Alaska is without a doubt, the prettiest place I ever seen.

On July 21, 1978, I married Debi. She is the best wife I could ever have. She has always been supportive of my military service. We had three kids, Jennifer, Jessica and Jake.

I have enjoyed remembering my experiences and writing about my life. God has been a big influence on my life. When I got away from his teachings, I would have hard times. I tried not to disappoint him, although sometimes I did. If you believe in Christ, and live according to his will, you will always be successful. I truly believe that.

I was told once that if you want to be successful, you must surround yourself with successful people. I think that is what I did by joining the Air Force and being part of it for so many years. Without a doubt, the finest people I have met were in the armed services.

The military taught me discipline and to take care of the things you are responsible for; integrity, to be honest and fair in all your dealings; compassion for all, no matter what race or color. And I think the most important thing above all, try to set the best example you can for others, always.

I would not be the person I am, nor been as successful, if it had not been for Debi and the kids. Debi has been the one that helped me through life because I did not want to disappoint her, although sometimes I did. I give all the credit to her, God, my parents and the U.S. Air Force Reserve.

JACK WERNER
United States Army

This is a letter that I wrote to one of Roger Crunk's daughters many years ago. It will explain itself.

"Hello, Kaitlin,

You wanted me to jot down some information, some memories, about your dad and our time together in Vietnam. It has been delayed long enough. We were K Co., 75th Airborne Rangers, assigned to the IV Infantry Division, stationed in the Central Highlands of South Vietnam. Words, phrases, names and nicknames come flooding back: Rock n' Roll, Drew, Angel, Mike, frag, free fire zone, NL ... and, always, Crunk.

Roger Crunk was a U.S. Army Ranger LRRP Team Leader right down to his marrow. He was a volunteer (we were pretty much all volunteers for the outfit); what I mean is that he volunteered us for every mission where volunteers were requested. He'll probably try to tell you that he never volunteered for anything. Bull! One way or the other, he let the First Sergeant know that he could count on us, if volunteers were needed.

Roger Crunk, 30 days after I was medi-vaced out, was machine-gunned in both legs while going back into the enemy fire zone for another team member who was already dead or dying. I don't think it would have made a lot of difference to your dad; I mean, that I think he would have walked straight into hell (that's what a killing zone was) just to retrieve a dead body. He didn't leave team members behind, dead or alive. When both legs were shattered with machine gun fire, he dragged himself the rest of the way and sat beside the downed Ranger, trying to stuff his guts back into his body with one hand while firing at the enemy with the other. We all knew that it was not idle words when Crunk said, "We all come back, or none of us do."

A U.S. Army Ranger is much more than endless training and hard muscles and courage; it is a love and a devotion that I have seen in few families. Kaitlin, if I wrote the dictionary, when you looked up the word Ranger, there would be a picture of your dad."

50 years is a long time to remember things. You do remember them, but in strobe light fashion. Some things that seem trivial, like lighting C-4 to heat LRRP rations, you remember with clarity. The 40 or so guys that you knew well in two years "in country" and you were certain that you would never forget, you do not remember most of them. Sure, those guys on your team and a handful of others that you have seen or communicated with, you know their names and their faces, but I wonder if I would recognize them (I don't think I would) if we had not seen each other through the years: Angel, Drew Fatten; Roger Crunk; Harry Phair "the Rock", Boatman, Chestnut, Gonzalez, Tipton,

Walker, Hernandez, Fields, Nguyen, Ray Allen, and so many more.

The first Ranger reunion that I went to, I called home and said it looked like a prosthetics convention. It appears to me that we have a higher divorce rate (3 for me) than the norm, but that is just an observation, nothing scientific. I think maybe a little higher suicide rate, too, but nothing that seems out of line. The suicides that I think I know about felt okay. A couple had long-term debilitating diseases, another was after a lengthy marriage and then a divorce. People do not accept suicide well, but it has always seemed like a valid, if not the best, option in some cases. I would kind of expect Rangers to lead the way. Every man was a volunteer for the unknown, for possible death or disfigurement; it has always been reasonable to personally own suicide as an option. No, I do not consider myself suicidal, but I damn sure own the option.

What was it like? I think the part that the books and movies have a hard time communicating is the all-encompassing daily battle with heat, body sores, rotting hurting feet, torn fingernails, leeches, diarrhea, feeling like you always had the flu, a raw burning rectum, zits/boils, filth, no shower, your sweat pouring so profusely that it was hard to hold your weapon or to see through glasses streaked with sweat and never anything dry to clean them on. The movie, *Hamburger Hill*, showed a little with the mud and the rain.

Who went to Vietnam? The average age was 19. If mummy and daddy paid your way through college, you did not go. Exceptions, of course—that is why they are called exceptions. Black kids went in huge numbers compared to white kids, until the public hell-raising put a stop to it. Wars are necessary, wars are important, wars are glorious--why, wars are a wonderful opportunity for blacks and Mexicans and poor whites. You see, the well-off don't have to serve. The very fact that they are well-off should tell you that they are too important.

I could not have served with better men, every one a volunteer. Ranger units tend to be elite and we, by definition, chose to be where we were. I speak of and for the common soldier, the backbone of our military. Would we have a better military if we required compulsory service for everyone? I don't know, but we would darned sure have a better country, a fairer county where everyone really had some skin in the game.

Politicians that have never served their country claim a life of "public service." Why do we vote for people who have not served?

What great insight do I have about war? About the Vietnam War? War will be embraced by decision makers. For politicians, it is power and self-importance. For big business, it brings wealth. Demand is at a constant high and price is seldom argued. Those making the decision to go to war and their progeny will not have to go to war. Should they so choose, they will seldom be in danger or discomfort.

Did the Vietnamese want us there? No. They wanted peace. They wanted to be left alone. Would they have gotten those things if the U.S. had not gone into Vietnam? No. North Vietnam and communism would have taken over sooner. I believed in the domino theory back then (the theory that if we let this country fall, then communism will move to the next). I no longer do and, worse, I do not even care if it is true. It is time we stop sacrificing our young men for other countries. We should not go to war unless we, or a specific predetermined treaty ally (i.e., Canada or England), is attacked. We do not need to be the policeman of the world. We should no longer participate in NATO or the UN unless and until all participating countries pay their full agreed-upon share and supply the agreed number of soldiers. We may be horrified by mass murder in Zimbabwe or Kuwait, but are you willing to send your child into it?

PTSD and the trauma of war: Does PTSD exist, is it a horror for some? Yes and yes, but it has become a buzzword, a victimization, an excuse for not accepting responsibility for getting on with our life. Child abuse, parental neglect, deformity, developmental disabilities, tragedy exist, but all the people exposed to these things are expected to get on with their lives as best as they can. Offer the veteran full medical care and counseling, but this crap of sitting around in groups telling each other how horrible the war was 30, 40, 50 years later is bullshit, especially when we have all our arms and legs (whole bodies). Lots of people who have not been to war have suffered horrible tragedies — the loss of a child, of a mate, a loved one with Alzheimer's. The psychologists that make a living out of PTSD would not agree with me, but the best advice, in my opinion, was "Suck it up. Get on with your life."

If it sounds as though I do not believe in counseling, that is not true. I think soldiers have the responsibility to seek it out on their own, and the military or VA should provide it. In my opinion, it should be private and personal. I question the vet that cannot get a job because "all he knows how to do is kill" or that he just cannot cope with trauma. You and I have seen civilians cope with unimaginable trauma and get up and keep going. I do not believe that the soldier that did the most or saw the most is usually the one out front talking about his/her PTSD.

What we focus on grows. Vets should be focusing on what they can contribute at work, at the homeless shelter or citizen committees, with the Boy Scouts, in their professional organization. I think there was a powerful reason that our fathers and grandfathers did not talk about the war. We regularly hear eulogies that tell of their heroic service which we knew little or nothing about. They came home wanting to focus on where they were GOING, not where they had been.

I know, for many of us, perhaps most of us, there is the feeling that this was the most important thing I ever did. At least, it was the time when I felt the most valued, the most important I've ever felt. I know that there was guilt when we returned whole and others did not. I know there was/is inexplicable anger, especially when no "victory" can be seen, but in the end, we are each in charge of our attitude, of our direction. No one can be better than a vet (war or no war experience) at focusing on making our community, our state, our country a little better place. Let us focus on what we want this place to be for our children and grandchildren. Let us lead the way in contributing to a better world in some small way every day. Try mine. I pick up trash every day, no matter where I am. It does not count if it is on my property, but everywhere else does: the Walmart parking lot or alongside the rutted road in Costa Rica. It makes me feel good. Every day. Try it.

Remember our vets? Yes, Veterans' Day, Flag Day, Memorial Day, July 4th. Yes, remember a veteran. Do more than one little thing, do two or three. Put out the American flag. Adopt the grave of a veteran that you do not know and clean it, put a small flag on it. Call Grandpa and say thanks for helping keep us free. But, above all, VOTE every time you have a chance. In war or at home, I have always equated my service with two things: the American flag and voting. Please value and respect our flag and please vote.

JASON KING
United States Army

The summer of 1992 changed things for me forever. My life, perspective and general view of the world did an about face in just a few short months.

With that said, this is not a tale of valor or anything remotely resembling heroism, but is a humble accounting of a naive boy from a small town being introduced to the reality of the wider world in a rather abrupt fashion.

I grew up poor in a small town of about 3,000 people whose claim to fame is a folk singer by the name of Woody Guthrie. That's right ladies and gentlemen, Okemah, Oklahoma. Oh! Never heard of it? I am not surprised. Typical small-town America, I suppose. Not much going on, but in those days, it was football and God...in that order. I mention this to help you better understand the culture shock I did not yet know I was quickly approaching.

Career day junior year of high school, to be honest I don't remember much about it except for the Army recruiter. I listened to his spiel feigning interest with no intent of joining, but hey, he offered to take me to lunch so I had to be polite. Well, a year and a few meals later, I was enlisted. I must admit the selling point for me was the incentives around helping me pay for college. Regardless of the reason, it was now done.

17 years old, a couple weeks after High School graduation, I was in route to Ft. Jackson, South Carolina. On a bus alone with my thoughts, I remember being scared that I wouldn't be able to handle it physically. After all, I had seen movies about how hard it was and this point in my life my perception of things was, well let's just say a little off. I expected everyone to be squared away and that I would be in the company of people I would struggle to keep up with. Keep in mind back in 1992 the Internet, while it existed, was not what it is today. I didn't even have a computer, let alone $6.95 an hour to connect to AOL On-line, and back then cell phones came in bags or were the size of a brick and texting didn't exist. Anyway, let's just say information wasn't quite as easy to come by, so I had television, the library, and people from whom to try and gain insight into what I was about to embark upon. I would say people were the main source from which I based my preconceived notions, but the problem with that is people are full of shit. Some good intentioned and some not so much, in the end you just have to read between the lines and go with it, and that is where I was, in deep thought, on a bus and then I arrived.

One of the things that I didn't have a particularly strong concept of upon arriving, is things are done for reasons that may not be logical or apparent to a newly arriving enlistee. Now, I consider myself intelligent, and I am both pragmatic and a logical thinker, so it is natural for me to try and "help" when I see things that could be done "better". I also come from a small town where, for the most part,

126

everyone is friendly. Normally these two things go together like peanut butter and chocolate, but in this particular situation, not so much. I imagine you can see where this is going and I will also say it only took a few instances for me to adjust my bearing, fall in line and keep my mouth shut.

At this point, as we exit the bus we are headed to reception, everyone in civilian clothes, no one knows what the hell is going on other than a lot of yelling and what seems to be chaos, when in fact and unbeknownst to us grunts, or to myself anyway, was it's all planned out and we are in for a long night. Now off the bus, and me thinking I have made the biggest mistake of my life, we are supposed to be lining up. People are already starting to get the idea that being quick about whatever is being yelled is probably prudent and after a few minutes we are lined up to the Drill Instructor's satisfaction. Yeah right, remember I said I was pragmatic, this is one of those times being logical is not a skill that needs to be exercised. Now, I am not stupid and I did not verbally respond, but when he told us to get back on the bus, that we had taken too long, I guess my expression, like a puppy tipping his head, was enough. This is when I started to believe that this gentleman did not much care for me, and it also happens to be the exact moment I learned that the brim of a drill sergeants hat is a terrible thing to behold.

My recruiter assured me over the course of our many visits that the DI's were not allowed to beat the crap out of us and up to this point I was about

75% convinced he wasn't lying to me. But that number quickly started to erode. The DI never actually "touched" me but the brim of his hat "Jackie Chan'ed" the shit out of my forehead. I was soon convinced pausing to ponder an instruction from a DI was a quick way to become popular! As I am writing this, I am smiling thinking how comical this must have looked, but at the time assure you I was terrified.

So, once my lesson was completed and we got on and off the bus a half-dozen times or so, we were finally led off to start the whole reception process. I do not remember what all we did that first night, I just remember we got finished about 45 minutes before wake-up call, and we were given the option to bed down for 45 minutes or we could shower early and get a head start. That first night was the roughest by far of the whole week-long reception process, and I think that is the whole point. I thought I was truly in hell when I first arrived. The remainder of my stay here was as follows: Move with all haste to point "A", wait for 2-5 hours then fill out 17,000 forms during which time you will write your social security number at least a half-million times. This process is repeated many times over the next week until you are all ready and prepped to go meet the nice gentlemen and ladies who will teach me to become a soldier over the next 10 weeks.

At some point during that week-long buzz saw of confusion and "hurry up and wait", I lost all my hair. Those damn clippers must have been 200 degrees and I am convinced the sadistic stylist operating them will have a special place reserved in hell for his services. In addition to becoming folically challenged, we learned the basics of how to behave and were given a good idea of what to expect through basic training.

Expecting a bus, I am now ready to go, feeling better now that I have acclimated a bit, the shock has worn off and I am squared away. We are all lined up and waiting and what the......

So maybe I spoke to soon. Bus you say? Nay, nay, enter "deuce and a half" stage left. Chaos ensues when some angry men exit these enormous trucks inquiring as to why our stuff and our asses were not already loaded. This went rather quickly as we have had a week to assimilate to the culture. And we were finally off. I think we must have driven around the base a few dozen times because it took an unusually long time to go a half mile, but eventually the trucks stopped and the yelling started. We all grab duffel's and pile them up and get into formation. We were yelled at for a while and instructed as our names were called to grab our duffel bags from the pile and report to one of four different platoons. This went off well and after a while, now operating as a company, we were taken into the barracks to unpack. Go Wolfpack!

Now first off, in the military you lock up everything, and a duffel bag is no exception. After about the 10th failed try on that godforsaken combination lock, panic started to settle in. Everyone else was already happily packing stuff into lockers and I'm the idiot who forgot his combination. That's what the panic was saying, but I knew the combination, what the hell is going on? That's when I noticed it wasn't my duffel bag. Now I know if you're reading this, you are probably thinking "you idiot". Yep, I would agree if it were that simple, but this glorious tale grows richer. It just so happens that at this spectacular junction in history, not only did one Jason King enter basic training on the same day, at the same base, in the same battalion, in the same company, but 2 of us did. At least we were in different platoons! Although I must own up to a little idiocy. The duffels were stenciled with First, Last and Middle initial as well as Social Security Number. What a joyful moment that was, realizing I have to go tell the DI I have the wrong bag.

To be fair, statistically this was crazy and I think that helped my, and/or our, situation. Yes, we got yelled at and made to feel like walking piles of incompetence, but it was apparent the DI's were entertained with the situation. Unfortunately, that was strike one. I'm sure you have probably heard: don't volunteer, don't stick out, all of that good stuff. Well, in less than an hour, I blew that possibility all to hell. Strike two came shortly thereafter, and strike three less than a week later. I now have zero chance of being a wall flower and it only gets worse.

That evening, once settled in, we were gathered for mail call. This was the first day and no one had mail but they did it anyway and explained how it would work in the future. In lieu of mail, we all had to give a quick introduction: name, age, and where we were from. Yep, here comes strike two, no way to avoid it, just get it over with. I was still 17, it turns out I was the youngest not only in the platoon but in the entire company. On top of that, I am from Oklahoma, and boy did they have a field day with that little tidbit. Several incestuous, corn-pone, back woods country comments later, my first day of basic was complete! But wait, what about fireguard? O yeah, fresh on everyone's mind was the baby Okie from Muskogee. Thanks Merle for that first shift of fireguard and for being voluntold to pick 5 other guys for the duty on the first night. "No, I am not from Muskogee" was the only response I could muster, which only added to the hilarity.

The next few weeks went smoothly, never enough sleep and full of activity, but here is where we come to my third and final strike. I was blessed with quite a few good friends from high school, family that promised to write and a girlfriend, when all combined kept me supplied with a steady stream of letters. This by itself didn't draw too much attention. However, in conjunction with the outside world knowing it was my 18th birthday, which up to this point only a couple guys in my squad knew about, lead to a mail call fiasco.

The DI, when doing mail call, usually called your last name and threw the letter in your general direction. This worked beautifully, up until about my 6th piece of mail. I figured I would get a few and quite honestly at this point I was ecstatic, as I had 6 letters or cards to read. Nope, letter 6 was the end of "happy time", and I knew it. As the down-turned brim of the hat slowly began to rise in my direction, it was clear the focus had shifted from distributing the pile of mail to the Okie from Muskogee, who had received at least one too many letters. The already quiet room went silent, as the Drill Instructor gave me the "stank eye" and an almost imperceptible shake of the head. This, however, was the day I legally became a man and I would not be denied, so I gathered myself and stared back, which from his vantage point I imagine I looked like "sad Puss-In-Boots" from Shrek. Pushing on with my testosterone-boosted manhood confidence, I then did the only thing I could think of, I gave a helpless shrug. Surprisingly, he didn't say anything, but slowly shifted his attention back to the mail. I breathed a "silent" sigh of short-lived relief because when after his merciful decision to not humiliate me he did not go back to calling out names and throwing letters. After a few minutes of this, I was beginning to get nervous when at last he went back to calling out names and throwing letters. Relief ebbed in again, but I should have known he was playing possum. When has was about half way through the remaining stack he stopped, and looked up with an utterly evil smile and said, "let's play a game".

"Jesus help me, here we go", I thought, as I faced that awful glare directed my way. Now I knew, in some way, this was directed at me, but I was in high spirits. My first thought was there is a...no, my first thought was "I don't like games", my second thought was there is a lot of mail left, so we are probably going to have to do something unpleasant to get our mail, but at least I won't be alone. Guess what? I was half right.

"For the remainder of mail call", the overly chipper DI barked, "you will give me ten push-ups for each piece of correspondence you receive."

Now, I must pause here to give kudos to the numerous, inventive and clever ways that DI's devise to mind fuck you. In this simple instance, and just a few minutes, I have been through a happy-to-fear-and-back-again cycle three times, and although I don't know it yet, he hasn't even delivered the "coup de gras".

So back to where I left off, I must have visibly shown signs of my relief because when he saw me relax a bit his already larger than life evil grin grew. My thinking was, cool that's not too bad. I probably have a few more letters at most, 30 push-ups, no problem. That was until I saw his smile grow, and then it hit me like a brick in the face. You clever bastard, I thought, and even smiled because I knew the secret he was about to unload on me.

And then it began, King, King, King, King, King, King. I could feel the letters bouncing off my back as I was counting and beating my face with a big grin, all the remaining letters were mine, all 23 of them. Believe it or not, it was the high point of my basic training experience. The DI even told me happy birthday, along with everyone else, and it was almost like we were normal people for those few minutes to lights out.

Somewhere around week 4, just about everyone in our squad had been hired and fired as squad leader, but I finally got my chance and to my surprise I managed to hold on to it until graduation. After week 4, just about everyone had the drill down. We lost a couple of guys to section 8 along the way, but once we caught the rhythm it was relatively uneventful to the end. We had a few guys faint during graduation be meh, who didn't!

I suppose I could finish here, but I decided to include the "cookie" incident. Forgive me because I don't really remember when exactly it happened as it was almost 25 years ago. When we first arrived, we were warned not to have food packages sent to us. If, in our infinite wisdom, we chose to ignore this sound piece of advice and received such a package that we would be welcome to eat it all, at once. One might say that's not so bad, just have a small portion sent. It was made clear there is no good ending in any scenario, and I immediately sent dispatches home with the warning DO NOT SEND FOOD EVER!!!

So far so good, right? We're all set, no problem, and no, none of my devious friends sent me anything for a laugh; that's amazing now that I think about it. This incident was self-inflicted, but I promise it wasn't my idea. To understand how one such as myself could possibly be so stupid, let me explain a few things.

It's common with a basic training platoon that you have 3 Drill Instructors. The Lead DI is meaner than a rattlesnake and takes zero shit from anyone, just plain ruthless. The other two are by no means sweethearts, but may from time to time show a smidge of compassion when the rattlesnake is not around. You guessed it, here we go again. For some reason, I don't remember if we ever knew why, but the rattlesnake was gone for a week or so. Our other two conspiring DI's let us know this fact and said, "Hey, if you guys want to receive a package, make sure you get enough to share...blah blah...but whatever you do, make sure it arrives before the rattlesnake is back, because we will deny and crucify if a package comes when he is back." They even told us the day he would return!

Hallelujah, lalala, gonna have me some chocolate chip cookies, ohh yeah! We were allowed to make phone calls throughout basic, so I had the mail down to a science, the math was good, I could call tomorrow, receive my package and have 2 days to spare, no problem. Well you see, I did my brilliant math based on letter delivery time, and in my lust for chocolate chip cookies, I failed to recognize a box containing 5 dozen chocolate chip cookies would take longer to travel through the United States Postal Service than would a letter.

Mouthwatering on expected delivery day at mail call, everyone knows they are coming and everyone in the platoon will get one, so the mood is good. No cookies, somewhat of a letdown, but they will come tomorrow, no big deal.

Expected cookie day + 1, same drill for sure today. No cookies. Now, just a bit of worry, but surely tomorrow, not even a little panic yet as I am sure they will come tomorrow.

Expected cookie day + 2, last safe cookie day, if those damn cookies don't come today I know the rattlesnake is going to make me eat all 5 dozen cookies in front of everyone. Mail call time, why is there no large package, he is messing with me. Surely, they are here. No cookies. The whole damn platoon is laughing after mail call. They are sympathetic but I must admit, if it was someone else I would have laughed. I was in true despair, there is no way out, how do I even describe the feeling of knowing you are going to pay the price for something stupid 24 hours from now but can't do anything to stop it. Tomorrow I will have to eat chocolate chip cookies until I vomit, then eat some more. Well, this is awesome, no sleep for me tonight.

I lived this experience and did not see what was coming next. It's the closest thing to a fairytale ending I think I will ever experience in my lifetime, but I swear it's the truth. My fairy god mother just happens to have the same name as I do. Five minutes before lights out, the other Jason King knocks on the Barracks door with a box containing five dozen beautiful, I don't have to eat them all myself, chocolate chip cookies.

Now, when I started this story, I mentioned how this changed me. It wasn't so much the training that impacted me as it was the people. I believe you would be extremely challenged to find a more diversified group of Americans. Mix that in with a little dash of the same hell everyone is experiencing at the same time and many of those barriers that define our current culture: ethnicity, social standing, and even religion, seem to dissolve. Now of course this is my opinion, and based on my own experience, but I would not be the same man I am today without that bond, and shared experience from a melting pot of 48 individuals that I called brother.

JEREMY KELLER
United States Air Force

My name is Jeremy and I joined the U.S. Air Force at the end of the summer right after I graduated high school in 1991. There was never any talk of a college fund and I didn't really know what I wanted to do for a lifelong career, so thought I would join the military to learn a trade. The day my parents dropped me off at the Military Entrance Processing Station (MEPS) is the only time I have ever seen my father cry. It caught me by surprise and made me think "What have I gotten myself into here?" The tears in his eyes made me really think for the first time that my decisions and actions really do have consequences. My father had served in Vietnam with the 101st Screaming Eagles, and that was my plan early on, but my dad told me to use my brain more than my muscles and stressed joining the Air Force instead. That is in no way a slam to the Army, I have had many brothers in arms in the Army and I cherish them as I will get to later. So, I enlisted in the Air Force and off to boot camp I went. Never in my wildest dreams knowing how far from our little farm in Washington state I would go or what was in store for me.

The second I got to boot camp I was surrounded by almost 50 other boys that were all different than me. I say boys because that is exactly what we were, a bunch of scrawny boys that didn't have a clue. Some of us got along, and some of us didn't, but we learned quickly that regardless of our differences we were all on the same team. The drill instructors hammered it into us daily that we had to find a way around our differences, or better yet, use our differences to get the job done. I had prepared physically for boot camp by running, doing pushups, climbing ropes, etc. and was shocked that no one else in my flight had seemed to prepare and really weren't in shape to perform our required physical education requirements. At the beginning, we didn't work together very well. It was a lot of personal survival and keeping your head down so the instructors would not single you out. Because of this, we were pretty much failing as a flight. Everyone was only focusing on their own responsibility and not helping each other. After a couple of weeks, we got a new guy in our flight that had been hurt during training and washed out of his flight. After his recovery, he joined ours. Looking back, this was good for us. He had been further along in his training than we were, so it was easy for him to see what we were doing wrong and he knew that we needed to work together more. He had such an impact on our flight that I sometimes wonder if he wasn't put there on purpose by the training command to straighten us out. It was in boot camp that I got my first real look at the camaraderie in the military. We started helping each other out where we were strong. I was good at shining boots, so many nights I would find myself sitting out on the fire escape with a couple other guys shining a dozen different pairs of our buddie's boots while they folded clothes or cleaned or did whatever it was they were good at. We learned to play to our individual strengths and the entire flight became better for it.

Once I completed boot camp, I moved on to Technical School at Sheppard AFB, Wichita Fall, TX for Inside Plant Telecommunications. I was to be a programmer on the base telephone system. There was a little more liberty there, so we got to hang out more off duty and started building relationships with those in our class and the others in our squadron. I was there the longest, so it was recommended I take a leadership role and become a Rope (a leader that had a colored rope over his right shoulder). We had 1 Red Rope over the squadron, Yellow Ropes had a floor that consisted of 4 hallways in a square, and a Green Rope was in charge of each hallway. I started as a Green Rope and was later promoted to Yellow. We had lines we had to rehearse and we were responsible for picking up the newly arrived recruits, getting them settled and making sure they knew the rules. Here it is, 24 years later, and I can go through old photos and still remember names and things we were doing at the time. I remember my buddy Bowman. That's another thing, we always used last names, so I honestly do not recall many of my friends' first names. Bowman is the guy I hung out with most in Tech School. I listened to nothing but country music and Bowman listened only to heavy metal. I remember when we left, we got each other gifts. He bought me the Metallica Black CD and I bought him the new Garth Brooks CD. When I left Wichita Falls, TX, I never saw Bowman again. I don't know how long he stayed in the military or what he ended up doing with his life, but I think of him often and smile as I remember listening to Metallica at the Shoppette while eating a slice of that greasy pizza they served.

I got my first assignment at Barksdale AFB in Louisiana. From the moment I was picked up at the airport, I was the part of a team. I was a Wire Dawg!! The two airmen who picked me up were so happy to see me! They grabbed my gear and took me to a government truck that transported us to the base. I was taken directly to the Enlisted Club where I met the rest of my "Dawg Pack". To be inducted into the pack I was required to drink a coffee cup of a putrid moving ooze. I was under age, so my drink did not have alcohol in it, something that I learned later was much more desirable than the non-alcoholic drink I was given. There was a major speech by our Non-Commissioned Officer In Charge (NCOIC). He told me that in the bottom of my coffee mug was a Wire Dawg coin, and after consuming all my drink, I could claim it and would officially be a Wire Dawg. I was informed afterward that some of the chunks in my drink were left over chili and the minty flavor came from toothpaste. Yes, it was that bad!!

I think the most memorable thing to me about the military was the camaraderie. The coin I received on that first night was to be my license. It was required to be within arm's reach at all times. Any time it was pulled out and seen by any other Dawg (usually by throwing it out on a table) it was considered a Coin Check. A Coin Check requires that every Dawg present must show their coin. If there is someone that is unable to present their coin, they must buy a round of drinks. If everyone present has their coin and shows it, then the person that started the coin check must buy the round. I would receive more coins throughout my tours, but none held a higher place than my Wire Dawg coin. My crew was my lifeline. We worked together, played together and even cried together occasionally. No matter what situation I was facing, I knew my Wire Dawgs had my back. And it wasn't only our squadron. I had many brothers/friends in other squadrons and even other branches of the military. In Guam, we hung out at Big Navy. It was the largest military installation in Guam and therefore had better shopping and clubs. I also hung out with the Patriot Battery Army guys on Guam, particularly a guy named Dumpster. Once I asked Dumpster if I should be worried about all the talk about SCUD missile launches. He looked at me and went dead serious. He said "Katfish, it is my job to intercept any SCUD coming into our area, and I am really good at my job. No, you have nothing to worry about."

Obviously, we did a "little" drinking in the military...scoffs!! But regardless of how drunk I got, I knew someone would ensure I got back to my rack to sleep in the safety of the barracks. Sometimes, I was the guarding angel. I've carried more than one brother back from the NCO club, back from A-Town in Korea and did the dreaded "Death March" from the main gate after the busses stopped running. We protected our own, meaning that no one was allowed to molest our charge while they were in their present condition. However, that does not mean we were not allowed to mess with our charge!

I remember a time when we came back from the NCO club and found an unlucky airman passed out in the door way to his room. Like good friends, we scooped him up and put him to bed. We then left one person to guard him until we returned. We promptly went off post, wrangled up a sheep and brought it back to his room. We then stripped him naked, put him to bed and left the room. He awoke the next morning to "Baaaaa" and he was naked, not remembering anything that happened the night before. Obviously, it was all done in fun and nothing happened between him and his new love, but he didn't know that! Oh, and by the way, the sheep was returned unharmed the next day. I once woke up to find both my arms had been shaved, not entirely just one swath across each forearm! For anyone that has actual siblings, you will understand some of this "I can mess with them but no one else can" ideology.

Even the knuckleheads were accepted. We looked out for them like they were a dumb little brother. I remember a time in Korea when an accident caused the base telephone system to crash. Virus and I went into "fix it mode" and started bringing it back online. It was a bad system crash and it took us hours to get even the priority lines up and weeks to fix all the minor problems. During the fix, the base was thrown in to an exercise to test our readiness capability. One night, after working a 17-hour shift, Twinkie started giving me a hard time about the system still having bugs and not working correctly. We were in MOPP gear and tired. We started arguing and he shoved me and I fell into a satellite dish display knocking it off its base. I got up and bounced him off a few walls and everyone jumped in and broke it up. A few minutes later, we were standing before the on-duty commander. When the commander asked Twinkie what happened, he stated that it was just a disagreement and that we were both coming off a very long shift and were tired. The commander asked me if that was it. I agreed that it was. And that was it. Twinkie and I never had another issue between us. I don't ever remember anyone holding a grudge in the military. If there was an issue, we dealt with it immediately so we could continue as a team.

In our squadrons, particularly in the mobility units, we all had nicknames. Now rule number one, you cannot pick your own nickname. Rule number two, the more you fight your nickname, the harder it will stick! I got a little lucky with mine. When I first got to Korea, I had just come off leave that I spent fishing with my father. So, I kept telling fishing stories. The guys picked up on that right away and determined my name was either "Basshole" or "Katfish". Can you guess which one I picked? I promise it was not Basshole! So, I was dubbed Katfish, my work partner was Crack Smoker and some of the rest were Virus, Phantom, Gipper, Volms, Sex, Huggy Bear, Kitty Kat, Brown Eye, JB, Slog, Junior and a plethora of others. I had no idea that my nickname would still be with me twenty some years later or that it would follow me from base to base! When I finished my tour in Korea, I was assigned to Elmendorf AFB, Alaska. I went home on leave, spent some time with the folks and finally caught a redeye to Anchorage. I stepped off the escalator in the baggage claim area and big black man approached me and asked, "Are you Katfish?" Now, how in the world did someone know my nickname here? Well, Kitty Kat also transferred from Korea to Elmendorf, just 4 months or so earlier, and there you have it. But, it gets weirder! About 4 years ago, after I had been out of the military for over 10 years, I went to a Halloween party at my niece's house. I was in the garage with a beer watching a beer pong game and someone shouts "KATFISH!!!" at the top of their lungs. Well, no one had called me that for quite a few years so obviously it took me by surprise. My head jerked up to find the source of the yell and standing in the doorway to the garage is Eddie Bauer, not the real one mind you, but Scott from Alaska! It was so good to reconnect after so long. And yes, I did throw a coin check on him and he got me a drink!! A few weeks later, he got in a situation and he needed help to get out of it. I drove almost 50 miles and cancelled dinner plans to go help move him out of a house that had a meth lab in it. That's just how we roll. When a Dawg needs help, other Dawgs show up to help.

In Alaska, Lou Dawg held us all together. He was one of the bosses, but also a friend to all of us and we normally partied at his house so he could keep an eye on us and keep us out of trouble. His wife, Pat, would put a pot of sausage and meatballs in a marinara sauce all day so we could have a good meal before we got stupid! Most of us would stay the night at his place, dibs on the couch or on his floor somewhere. I didn't drink much in those days, so it would always bother him to realize I was gone. He would call me at home and chastise me for driving in my condition. I had to explain that I had not been drinking and was sober. I love that man for always checking up on us. I was adopted by two different families in Alaska. Steve and Erika were my NASCAR family, and John and Adelia were my Thanksgiving family. That wasn't the only times we got together, but the most memorable. On Saturday night, I would go to Steve and Erika's house and the next morning she would make us breakfast and we would watch NASCAR. They taught me all the rules and who the good drivers were and how to follow the race. So many good times. I hope they know how much it meant to me to share that time, to have a place to go that wasn't work or my lonely studio apartment. Every Thanksgiving I went to John and Adelia's house. I learned that John had a tradition to always watch John Wayne's McClintock on Thanksgiving and I still hold that tradition at my house. His kids called me Katfish and even searched me out on social media to be friends! I even got school graduation invitations, marriage invites and baby announcements from some of them. My wife and I were not able to have children of our own, so it means a lot to me that I am still in contact with my buddy's kids. They somehow feel like mine.

Every time I left a base and had to say goodbye to friends that had carried me, cried with me, fought beside me, I told them that if they ever needed me I would be there for them. When I left Guam, I went to the shop in the middle of the night before I left and wrote this quote on the white board, "A man can be hard to find in the mountains, but y'all are welcome at my campfire anytime!" In Guam on an airman's last country night at the club, they would always play Alabama's "Goodbye-Kelly's Song" as a dedication to those leaving. Picture 40-50 people in a circle on the dance floor, arms around shoulders, singing this song. It was very hard. These men and women you have spent the last year, 15 months, 2-3 years with, meant the world to you. And the chances of you seeing them again is so rare. I have seen 3 of my old service buddies in the last 14 years since I separated, and that's a lot. I had a very dear friend in Guam that kept me out of a lot of trouble. His name was Wes and we ended up going to San Antonio together also. But after that, I went to Korea and I think he went to New Mexico and I haven't seen him since. I tried to find him on social media but to no avail. Wherever he is, I pray he is doing well. I hope he got married and had some kids. I also hope he looks back at the times we shared and smiles as he remembers fishing in Canyon lake, teaching me to eat rare steak with a glass of red wine at the NCO club or SCUBA diving off Gunn Beach in Guam. I think of my brothers often and always with a smile and a prayer. A prayer that each one of them knows they will hold a place in my heart for the rest of my life.

JILL DODSON HALE
United States Army

20 years seemed like a lifetime when I joined the Army back in 1991! I still remember getting the call from the recruiter, deciding college wasn't for me, and meeting him to discuss my options. He showed me a video of Soldiers jumping out of planes, and I was hooked! When I went to the MEPS station, I remember their surprised looks as I requested to be airborne. My first time on a plane was my flight to basic training in Fort Jackson, SC. My second time on a plane was my first jump!

My first recollection of beginning airborne school was that there were only a handful of females. Most of the girls were tough as nails. We had to keep up with the males; no exception! My second recollection at the school were the Black Hats! They were mean and tough and didn't take excuses—not that I was going to give any!

Everywhere we went, we ran! I remember one specific run where a Black Hat was on my tail, asking me if I was going to quit. "Quit, leg!" "You can't handle it!" "You wanna be a leg?" The word "leg" was a cuss word in airborne school!! You did not want to be a leg (non-airborne soldier); you weren't allowed to associate with legs; and definitely couldn't marry a leg!! I look back at that run, with that Black Hat on my fourth-point-of-contact, and know that he was motivating me!

After graduation (which was held after the fifth jump on the jump zone, and my airborne wings were pinned on me by an old airborne guy), one of the Black Hat's pulled me aside and asked me where I was going. I told him I was going to Fort Bragg, North Carolina, and he told me to request the 82nd Airborne Division. He either had a lot of respect for me or wanted to see me fail; I'll stick with the first one!

Once I got to the reception station at Fort Bragg, I immediately told them I wanted to go to the 82nd; and they laughed and laughed! I mean, who is this chick Private coming in here still wet behind the ears, asking to go to the 82nd? For some it's a punishment, for others it's a goal! My wish was granted, and I was shipped over to the 82nd Reception!

I realized early on that I was one of a handful of females throughout the organization. I went to 82nd Signal Battalion, one of a few that had women. In the barracks, I roomed by myself for a while, and then more women trickled in.

It wasn't long into being there that I met my first husband, who at the time was a Specialist. He was in my section, where we worked on secure radios and equipment. He was a professional with aspirations to go Special Forces. His Soldiers would follow him anywhere, which spoke a lot of his leadership skills! One of my friends and I were always together (still friends to this day, 25 years later, thanks to social media); I was still new, so I was likely to follow those I knew like a lost puppy. Everyone thought me and Al were an item due to this friendship, which was fine considering my future husband was also my squad leader.

As a new Soldier and a female, I had a lot to prove. I'd do the hard jobs without whining; learn to drive the deuce-and-a-half like a pro, and pushed myself physically to keep up! I struggled a lot with my running, even though I could easily run an 8- or 9-minute mile — it just wasn't enough to keep up with the guys! We'd regularly run 4 miles for PT (physical training), and sometimes be surprised by the commander and/or first sergeant and run sometimes 8, sometimes 10 miles!

We used to say (and maybe they still do) that the 82nd has the fittest alcoholics in the Army! We would regularly drink to excess and get to sleep in the very early hours of the morning, only to roll over a few hours later and run our butts off! We took PT tests every 6 months, and took diagnostic PT tests quite often. Those didn't count for record, but could assess how a Soldier was doing. I remember one time taking a diagnostic PT test with my section, and listening to all the guys shit talking back and forth; then it was my turn! I busted out 70 pushups in 2 minutes; it rattled them and they got quiet! They knew they couldn't get beat by a girl! Needless to say, I could challenge them every once in a while!

Going to the field was a little trickier for me! I was scared of the dark (yes, I was 20 and did eventually grow out of it)! They'd send me out for guard duty, and I'd hear and see things the whole time! I was much happier when I was in that foxhole with one of my buddies! But I always tried to pull my weight otherwise. Plus, I was always good at following orders! So, if they said jump, I'd jump!

Looking back, I miss the ruck marches! Our section would go out once a quarter to ruck 12 miles (in 3 hours, I think). We did it as a team, and we'd push each other the whole way through! This was another thing I excelled at. Not because of my strength or endurance, but because I wouldn't give up, and I'd push through every step to keep up with the guys. These were always special to me, but my body would hurt from top to bottom for days after, in muscles I didn't even know I had. I did struggle with sensitive feet, and therefore spent much of my 2 years there with blisters on my heels.

There were differences that I tried to, but couldn't, ignore—besides the physical aspect and my fear of the dark. My section had a "war box" that went with us when we went to the field. It had pictures of naked or half-naked women. I didn't make a big deal about it, but at some point, one of our leaders did, and the porn show had to go! I was more embarrassed that they took them down because of me, than I ever was of those pictures.

Also, there was the 'pink belly' that was given to some unlucky guy who was celebrating a birthday or a promotion. They'd hold down the guy, and everyone in the section would slap his belly as hard as they could, leaving welts and, well, a pink belly. It was all in fun, of course; but I was never initiated by this brotherly act of love.

And men from other units within the 82nd would look at me with either disdain or longing; looking back, I can't decide which was worse. Back then, the look of disdain bothered me more. They'd even ask, "We have women in the 82nd?" Unless they worked with me or knew my reputation, they assumed the worst. As a young Soldier, that bothered me terribly! Today, I'd shrug it off and carry on.

I even had the 'rare' occasion where I'd have to hear about how a man doesn't believe women should be airborne or even in the Army! I'd fight that tooth and nail, and spent many days trying to prove them wrong! I worked very hard to be accepted for what I could do; and ignored what they thought I couldn't do. I tried not to dwell on the fact that I was a girl, and felt most comfortable as just 'one of the guys".

I loved jumping out of airplanes, but I was never a fan of hurry-up-and-wait. They'd stick us in 'cattle cars' to take us to Pope Air Force Base, get us suited up with our parachutes and spare parachutes (if we were lucky! Normally, we jumped with a ruck sack between our legs and a rifle on our side); and then we'd sit around and wait, sometimes hours, for the weather to change or whatever else (I was still just a specialist by the time I left the 82nd and self-centered). This waiting game had to be the worst part about being a girl. If I had to pee, I had to take all of that off just to go. It was embarrassing, and the first time in my 20-year career where I wished I wasn't a girl. I would have given anything to just be able to whip it out! I felt that way several times in my career, but the second time where being a girl was super inconvenient was during my first deployment to Iraq.

I left the 82nd after a short 2-year tour due to my then-husband becoming Special Forces with orders for Okinawa, Japan. I loved my time at Fort Bragg and was sorry to leave. It wasn't until I in-processed in Japan that I realized just how much I missed it!

In the 82nd, no one would ever dream of failing a PT test or a weigh in; but I soon learned the rest of the Army did not hold the same standards. Yes, there were standards to meet, and if you didn't you'd be flagged (ineligible for promotions and awards); but it wasn't so taboo in my future units. I left the 82nd as a Specialist promotable, and soon after getting to Okinawa, I was promoted to Sergeant. At that time, I became the training NCO, and administered the PT tests, weigh-ins, and unit training events. It was certainly an eye-opening experience to go from 'the best of the best' to just barely getting by. Yet, I loved that unit and everyone after that as much as the 82nd.

However, the 82nd airborne shaped the kind of Soldier I was and the kind of leader I'd become. I credit my time with the 82nd for giving me the fortitude to handle everything else that came up in my 20-year career. This drive I developed in 82nd pushed me to progress quickly from specialist, to sergeant, to staff sergeant in my second unit, the 333rd Signal Company, in Okinawa.

At a very young 26, and only 6 years in the Army, I became a platoon sergeant in the 29th Signal Battalion at Fort Lewis, WA. Before that I was the shop foreman for the same section, the Electronics Maintenance Shop. I enjoyed both jobs, and my discipline learned in the 82nd allowed me to not stand for crap (aka BS) from my Soldiers! I hated when they were late to formation, and they'd learn that the hard way through pushups—and lots of them! I also learned to stand up for my Soldiers when I felt like they were getting the shaft. I often spent time butting heads with my cocky, misogynistic shop officer over treating them unfairly or making decisions without including my input. I realize as I'm writing this, just how much my airborne training and time with the 82nd set me up for success and a good career.

After being passed over for Sergeant First Class in a slow progression MOS like 29S/35E, where you only got promoted when someone retired or got promoted, I applied for Officer Candidate School. This was a second attempt for that as well, but I had that "don't quit, don't take no for answer" mentality. This time, I was at a larger base with a larger admin section that had a recipe for success - I also had 90 credit hours of college versus the 60 credit hours I had at the time of my first submission, and I was accepted! I was elated and assumed I'd be joining the best of the best at Fort Benning. Boy was I in for a surprise! Yes, there were a lot of stellar NCO's there, but I quickly found out that not everyone was top notch. We had some that came straight from Basic Training, and several of them were lacking the skills necessary to be an officer, let alone a specialist.

I went in the OCS with a special mindset of 'this is just a game'. After being a respected NCO and staff sergeant, it was definitely an adjustment to being a candidate! And like everywhere else, there was jealousy from some. One cadre in particular, a minority woman and staff sergeant, who was out for blood. I took that, and other problems, in stride. I had always been a stellar NCO, and I was not about to let someone ruin my career out of jealousy. Also, the rigorousness of the program, both physically and mentally, challenged my entire being. Again, I look back to the start of my career in the 82nd, and I believe it was my time there that centered me for the craziness that came with OCS. I graduated one month after 9/11, and due to being locked down much of that month, I had no idea the pain our country had been in. I went to Officer Basic Course at Aberdeen Proving Ground, MD. Of course, this was a fun time for all of us lieutenants, but I think I especially had fun. I was newly divorced and ready for some fun! Of course, we had studying to do, and we'd get together for study time where I drank too much, but woke up to acing the test. This really irked my fellow LT's to no end, but again, my time in the 82nd, drinking and waking up to function at a high rate of speed, is to blame for this 'success'. I graduated first in my class taking <<Distinguished Honor Graduate>> and being awarded the <<Leadership Award>>.

Next stop, Hanau, Germany as the Force Protection Officer. My confidence and 'no BS' attitude afforded me the opportunity to excel in this position. As a second lieutenant, my battalion commander and battalion training officer entrusted me with protecting 5 small bases, or kasernes. Our battalion was on Hutier Kaserne, but there were 4 other small bases that needed the protection of our Soldiers. I checked on the soldiers regularly, made sure they were following orders and not taking short-cuts, because as I said — this was a new Army. The Army before OCS was a peace-time environment, but after the enemy had essentially declared war by taking down the World Trade Center, we were prepared for an attack, anywhere, anytime. It didn't run perfectly — what does, really? — but I had some great Soldiers and NCOs guarding our bases! They trusted me, and I relied on them! As a second lieutenant, I definitely had to prove myself with the NCO's, who had seen their fair share of shoddy lieutenants. But once I informed them of my history as an NCO, or they got the chance to work with me, I got their respect.

In early 2003, I was deployed with a small forward element to Kuwait. We took over camp mayor operations at one of the outlying camps in the desert, Camp Udairi. I was again the force protection officer, ensuring our camp was adequately protected. Holy sand storms, SCUD attacks, and dining facility fires!! A few months later, the rest of our battalion headquarters met up with us, and two days after the war started we were sent into Iraq. I can honestly say, that this was one of the few times where I was SCARED. We had just learned about the Jessica Lynch convoy being taken prisoner, so my mind was reeling!

I drove with a first lieutenant who I had spent the past few months with; she kept falling asleep! I was paranoid of what's going to be on our left and our right, so I kept waking her up. Her dad had sent her some dip, as a joke I think, but you better believe I was dipping to stay awake! But, the enemy was nowhere to be seen! We saw a lot of camels and burned out vehicles though! We did have some close calls with enemy forces the further north we drove, but no one shooting at us. We drove west of Baghdad to a petroleum refueling station ran by one of our companies. It was dark, but we could hear the mortars and gunfire all night long, so sleep was fitful at best. The next day, we headed back south to set up near Tallil Air Base. The first few nights were spent awake waiting on an attack, as intelligence had informed us that the enemy had plans to take us out. All was quiet though, and we eventually moved on to Dogwood, where we spent the rest of our year.

I was promoted to first lieutenant and moved to the 77th Maintenance Company, where I became the platoon leader for the largest platoon in the battalion. This was by far my favorite assignment in my 20 years. I loved the NCO's, Soldiers, and officers! So many stories, but my favorite is when, on my first night in the company, the platoon leader tent tried to blow away during a sand storm. Me and my buddies were holding that thing down to the best of our ability! We were on several convoys that were hit with IED's (or roadside bombs), but no one was seriously injured.

After a year as the platoon leader to the best group of Soldiers and NCO's, I moved to being the Maintenance Control Officer. I enjoyed this job immensely, but again dealt with some jealousy from a fellow lieutenant. Something I've learned from my years in the Army and beyond, is that strong women build each other up and don't tear each other down. I never experienced this animosity as an NCO, I don't know why it changed when I became an officer. Again, I persevered through this, but never understood the desire to tell lies about me.

I moved to the battalion S-4 (logistics) upon promotion to captain at the behest of my amazing battalion commander. Biggest problem there was that my beloved commander was leaving, and in his place, came a hurricane who made all her staff officers lives a living hell! I'm not going to waste time on this, but shortly after change of command, we deployed back to Iraq at the end of 2005. We took over operations from another CSB on Tallil Air Base. I spent a lot of time traveling to bring back vehicle fleets and equipment. I traveled either by air or by convoy, often the convoy commander. The rest of the time was spent on PowerPoint slides and reports. We did get hit a few times by RPG's, but we all survived. A few convoys of our companies were not quite so lucky.

After returning at the end of 2006, I was done with deployments and Germany. I headed to the advanced course in Fort Lee. After that, I requested a reprieve from deployments, and ended up in Oklahoma City, OK working with a reserve unit. I married and had a child, only to find out 5 months later, that I had thyroid cancer. After surgery and radioactive iodine, I was declared NED (no evidence of disease), but was nondeployable for a year after due to the side-effects of not having a thyroid.

Oddly, I consider the cancer a blessing as it led me to be assigned to a non-deployable unit in Rock Island Arsenal, IL for my final duty station before retirement. Nine months after the radiation, I was pregnant again with my youngest child. At the time of my retirement, I was significantly overweight due to 2 babies and cancer. As a proud airborne Soldier, this was an embarrassment, but I was still nondeployable, and there was a medical reason for my weight gain. I was thankful to be able to retire at 20 years--10 years enlisted and 10 years as an officer!

In my 5 years since retiring, I have lost 80 lbs., ran 2 marathons, 5 half marathons, and several shorter races. I divorced and remarried. I suffer from PTSD, anxiety, depression, back pain, thyroid hormone issues, fibromyalgia, arthritis, and alcoholism. Outpatient and inpatient treatment, relapses, hating myself, wishing I'd die, and now a renewed attempt at sobriety. I'm currently very early in this new sobriety, but today is different. I'm attending meetings (90 in 90), I have a sponsor, I'm working the steps, and trying to be of service to others. I volunteer at my kids' school, and I am in the process of signing up to volunteer with the local animal rescue and the Veteran's Center in town.

I still believe that my airborne training and time in the 82nd Airborne Division, set me on a great career path; with drive and motivation unknown to many, a disciplined mind, and a will to survive whatever has been thrown at me. I will be forever grateful for every experience in the Army, but specifically for those two very intense years as a young Soldier.

HOOAH! AIRBORNE! ALL THE WAY!

KEN ~~ARGUS~~
United States Army

I was in college in upstate New York. Not sure why. I didn't really want to be there. I didn't have a plan. All my friends went to college so I went to college.

I was close to home, and as a poor kid, financial aid paid for it. So, I guess it was ok, I had nowhere else to be. Girls, beer, repeat. Pointless, but what else was I going to do? What else did I want to do?

It was a Tuesday, October 25, 1983. I put in an Aerosmith cassette as I drove to the dorms. I parked the car and walked over to the building where my friends lived. I got in the elevator and pressed the button for the all-girl floor. As the doors opened, I stepped into chaos. Girls, some dressed, some not so much, were running up and down the hallway. Some were crying, some were screaming. I heard news stations being played on radios in the background.

"US Army Rangers have invaded the island of Grenada." Grenada?? Where's Grenada? None of the girls seemed to know either, but they were hysterical. "I have a friend in the Marines!! Oh my God! Is he alive!?!?" "Assholes! Why would they do that?!!" "Oh my God! Oh my God!" "Damn them!!" I didn't see what the problem was, but these college students were losing it.

As the day went on, some of the blanks got filled in. The politics of it didn't interest me much. American lives were safeguarded, sounded good to me. Army Rangers parachuting into combat?? Now, that got my attention. A plan was starting to form.........

It was a Friday at Ft Bragg, North Carolina. It had been over six years since that crazy day in the girls' dorm.

In that time, I had joined the Army and was serving in the Airborne Infantry, much to the dismay of my recruiter. He screamed at me when I turned down the computer jobs he offered me. I wanted to be a grunt. I wanted to jump into combat. That was the real Army. The recruiter continued to argue. I threatened to go to another recruiter. He angrily processed the paperwork. I had done what others wanted in the past, this time I was doing what I wanted.

After Basic Training and jump school, I had spent a year at 'Bragg and then headed over for a tour in Northern Italy. I had a number of accomplishments already. I was a Sergeant, and in addition to my jump wings, my uniform now possessed the coveted Ranger Tab. I had built a firm foundation as a soldier and I loved it.

We were on DRF-1. Division Ready Force #1. In the 82nd Airborne Division that means you need to be within 2 hours of the unit at all times. Your bags are packed. Your vehicles are palletized, waiting to be dropped from planes. If the calls come, you're it. Wheels up, headed anywhere in the world, ready to fight, within 18 hours.

Things in Panama had been getting tense. The country's leader, Manual Noriega, had lost the recent election, but refused to accept the results and said he intended to remain in power. His relationship with the U.S. had deteriorated badly, and he recently said a state of war existed between our two countries.

Today, Friday, Noriega's thugs had killed an American Marine Lieutenant! I believed this boiling pot had just boiled over, and we were on DRF-1!! I knew the call would come! I wanted the call to come!

Friday night, I went to bed without a call. Saturday, I stayed close to home, no call. Sunday...they had killed an American serviceman, AND STILL NO CALL!!!

Monday morning, I drove onto Post in disbelief. It had been 3 days since the Lieutenant had been murdered and America's rapid deployment force was still sitting on the ground. We ran PT, showered and had breakfast. At the 0900 formation, we marched down to the battalion headquarters area for a larger formation. At the formation, we were given information about the AUSA, (Association of the US Army) and encouraged to join. Suddenly, someone ran up to the speaker and informed him we had been activated. He ordered us to report back to our companies. The call had come!!

The Company Area was buzzing with activity. The official word was that we were going to perform an EDRE (Emergency Deployment Readiness Exercise). We would go through all the motions as if it were real, then we would jump onto Sicily Drop Zone on Ft. Bragg and spend a few days in the field. Sure. I didn't believe that for a second. I had waited all weekend for this call and it was real!

Soon I realized that people were believing what they wanted to believe. Guys like me, who wanted to go, believed the EDRE story was a smoke screen and we were going to Panama. Others, who didn't want to go, afraid perhaps, chose to believe the EDRE story; it was just training.

I knew it was real, but the clincher was when the 1SG passed down to the Squad and Section Leaders that their troops should wear jungle boots if they had them available. Jungle boots?! If we're staying in Ft. Bragg in late December, jungle boots would not be the recommendation. Panama, however, was much warmer, wetter and humid. Jungle boots make sense.

People around me continued to disagree with my theory as we loaded our gear into vehicles and headed to the PHA (Personnel Holding Area), a quanson hut type containment area for pre-deployment planning. As we got off the vehicles

165

and walked toward the barbed wire covered entrance gate, a flatbed tractor trailer pulled up, loaded with cases and cases of live ammunition!! No more debate. It was real.

The process began. Emergency contact information, check. Last Will and Testament, Power of Attorney, check. Dog tags, check.

The cute brunette medic told me to drop my pants and put my weight on one leg. The vaccine hurt much more than usual. Ok, other butt cheek. Damn that hurt!

With the administrative stuff covered, it was time for the meat and potatoes. Operation's Order, commo checks, MRE's, top off your canteens, ammunition. As with most missions in the military, you get your things in order and then you wait. You try to rest. It's been a busy day and a half. The Chaplain is walking around, talking to guys, praying with some of them. He's a young Lieutenant. New to the unit. He and I would end up going to war together on two different continents, and forming a relationship that exists to this day.

Ok, time to leave the PHA and walk over to "Green Ramp," the Air Force staging area. Wait, what's going on? Why, what? They need to scratch some of our guys from the jump to make room for others. Cutting a few from each Section is discussed, but eventually a Platoon Sergeant volunteers his entire platoon to stay back. He argues that is the simplest way to do it. He's already been to combat once and is nearing retirement. I think he may have other motives, but his logic makes sense. I recently transferred from his platoon to the one I'm in now. I trained those troops, they're sharp and motivated, but now they're furious. I would be, too. Imagine you're a football player. You train and train. You're mentally and physically ready. Then on game day, the coach says don't dress, you're not playing. Devastating.

As the line moves toward the door, a Private from the platoon that's staying behind walks up to me. "Sgt. Mes, do something cool with this." he says, with tears in his eyes, as he hands me a folded American Flag. "I will, Bake." I reply, as I put the Flag in a cargo pocket.

The walk to Green Ramp is short. Everyone is quiet. It's cold, windy and dark. Late Tuesday night. We line up behind our planes and lay down on the tarmac. We check our gear, then double check it. Then check it again. Everything is as it should be. So, we wait. I was doing ok with the cold, but now it's starting to rain, and the rain is turning to sleet. Miserable.

Time for parachutes. Word comes down to take off your "snivel gear." It's cold, but this will be the last chance to get rid of polypropylene under-garments before jumping into the tropics. It may be freezing at Ft. Bragg, but Panama will be a completely different story. I encourage my men that they'll be happy they did it 8 hours from now. One Staff Sergeant I know chooses to remain warmer and take his chances. He would end up spending the first three days of the conflict at an aid station receiving IV fluids as a heat casualty.

I make one more run to the fence line. It's a 5-hour flight. You know how you use the restroom on a combat loaded C-141 Starlifter? You don't.

Alright, parachute is on and inspected. C'mon guys, it's still sleeting out and we're sitting in it. I'm freezing! Cold sucks, wet sucks, but cold and wet really sucks! Thank God! Time to board. We waddle up the back ramp of the aircraft, one parachute on our back, one on our front, rucksack laying across our legs, rifle cased under the left arm.

I sit down. More comfortable than on the tarmac and grateful to be out of the weather. The heat circulating inside the plane slowly starts to warm me and dry my clothes. Waiting. I finally stop shivering. Why aren't we flying? We're told the wings of some planes need to be de-iced and we'll leave as soon as we can. The decision is made, we can't wait anymore. Send whatever planes are ready. I'm fortunate enough to be in the first wave of planes to leave. This will give me cover of darkness when I jump. My plane is airborne and I settle in for a 5-hour nap.

Don't think you could sleep on your way to war? You can. You better. Once you hit the ground, you don't know when you'll get to sleep again. I was tired and the cold had fatigued my body even more. I slept just fine. Good thing too, because for me, the pace wouldn't slow down for several days.

Twenty minutes! TWENTY MINUTES!! We're twenty minutes from drop time. Wake up. Ten minutes! TEN MINUTES!! The jump commands begin.

Get ready!
GET READY!
Outboard personnel stand up!
OUTBOARD PERSONNEL STAND UP!
Inboard personnel stand up!
INBOARD PERSONNEL STAND UP!
Hook up!
HOOK UP!
Check static line!
CHECK STATIC LINE!
Check equipment!
CHECK EQUIPMENT!
Sound off for equipment check!
SOUND OFF FOR EQUIPMENT CHECK!

OK! Ok! Ok...............All OK Jump master!!

Each of the jump commands are repeated and obeyed, just like so many training missions before. The pressure inside the aircraft changes. It gets louder and hot air rushes over us. The door is open.

Someone yells the DZ is hot. They're not talking about the air, they're talking about the bullets.

I'm struggling to stand upright. My ruck is too heavy. My arm is up holding my static line at a reasonable height, but the rest of me is folded down at knee level. I see a Lieutenant standing on a seat above me. "Hey Lt., let me know when the green light goes on." "Will do, Sergeant!"

1 MINUTE! 30 SECONDS! STAND BY!

"Green light Sergeant!!"

Finally, the wait is over. I feel the bodies around me start to shift. Moving, we're moving. I muster up all the strength I have to straighten up my weighted down body and push myself forward for the short distance to the door. Shuffle, shuffle...I can hear the wind, there's the door, I see water...WHOOOSH! I fall out into the early morning darkness over the Republic of Panama!

The mission calls for us to jump onto an airfield and secure it. In the Op Order, we were told the drop zone is 75% concrete. It is an airfield after all. I'm not encouraged. I've jumped onto airfields in training and I have the bruises to prove it.

I count to 4, my 'chute opens. Drop my ruck on its 18-foot tether. This is going to hurt. Knees bent, feet together...I'm on the ground in seconds, and there's no pain, no pain at all. I landed in grass! Fluffy, green grass!!

I'm in front of the terminal, just off the runway. I see a two-man Air Force Combat Control Team kneeling nearby. I move to them and kneel next to them. I need to find the vehicles that were dropped before us. During DRF-1, HMMWVs, tanks and artillery pieces are all pre-loaded, rigged to drop and just sitting in a guarded warehouse waiting for a war. One of them was mine.

"Did you guys see where the heavy drop landed?"
"Yep." he responded as he pointed, "Out there." I considered his words and the direction his arm was pointing.
I hoped I misunderstood. "That whole area is swamp." I said as more of a question than a statement. "Yep." he said, as he went back to his radio traffic.

10-foot elephant grass, water...ugh. After much effort, I finally see a chemlite glowing ahead of me. The Air crews activated chemlites on each of the heavy drop items before pushing them from the aircraft. As I approach the vehicle, I'm already wondering how I'll get it out. But all that wondering fades when I reach the chemlite and it's attached to 105 mm howitzer, not a HMMWV. I sit down on the howitzer, hot and tired. As I catch my breath, I hear something moving through the tall grass toward me. I lower my body behind the artillery piece for cover. I point my rifle toward the sound and quietly switch off the safety. As I decide between rifle fire or a 40mm grenade, the men walking in my direction speak...in English. The two men were Artillerymen looking for their howitzers.

Everyone was running into the same problems. We just improvised. Eventually, I ended up with an Engineer HMMWV. I know it was an engineer HMMWV because it was full of explosives, which engineers use to breech obstacles. Also, several days later, while driving on the airfield, an engineer Major spotted me and demanded his vehicle back. Oops. "Yes, Sir. Here you go, Sir. I've been looking for you."

While I was fighting elephant grass and improvising vehicles, other members of my battalion boarded Black Hawk helicopters and flew toward their target.

Operation Just Cause was a complex, multi-faceted mission. Every branch of the military and many different units were involved. Several different airfields were seized. Two different prisons were liberated. Bridges were secured, aircraft were destroyed. The Panama Canal was safeguarded. Noriega was hunted down and a new leader was installed.

After the airfield, my battalion's primary objective was Tinajitas. Tinajitas was a hill with a Panamanian Defense Force compound sitting at the top. Our troops would insert via Blackhawk, move up the hill and seize it.

As the helicopters approached the objective, PFC Denson took a bullet in one of his legs. Denson was from Texas; he wasn't going to be stopped. He insisted on exiting with the rest of his men rather than returning on the Blackhawk. On the ground, he was further wounded. Specialist Daves was also wounded fighting up the hill, and suffered fatal injuries from mortar fire while waiting to be evacuated. Both men died on that hill. Other troopers left pieces of themselves on that hill, but lived to tell of it.

I arrived at Tinajitas the next day in one of the many convoys that drove between Omar Torrijos Airfield and Tinajitas. Most of those convoys had been ambushed and several of the guys in my company had been injured and evacuated back to hospitals in the States. The top of Tinajitas was secure. As we settled in to defensive positions for the night, the Battalion Commander was checking on the troops. I approached the Commander and told him I had a present for him.

His serious face seemed quizzical, but not interested in jokes. I wasn't joking. I reached into my cargo pocket and presented him with the American Flag that I had jumped in. He was surprised, but seemed pleased and walked away without saying anything else.

The next morning, at a short memorial service, we assembled in formation and raised that American Flag over blood stained Panamanian soil in tribute to two of our own. When I made that promise back at the PHA, I had not envisioned this. Watching Old Glory waving in the sunny sky over Tinajitas, I felt I had kept my promise. I hope Daves and Denson would agree.

In total, Just Cause would cost the United States 23 men. All objectives were completed, all missions accomplished. We made our way home. Noriega made his way to a prison cell. Daves, Denson and 21 others made their way to rest in friendlier soil.

Like many veterans before me, when I celebrate Memorial Day in May, it's not generic. My Memorial Day will forever have names attached.

MATTHEW BALLANTYNE
United States Army

In a ramp up to combat, strange things happen on an Army base. Especially when soldiers know their time is coming. That their safety and comfort within the United States is about to end, because their unit is being sent thousands of miles away, because the anticipation lingers, I begin to think are the reasons that some soldiers begin to act out of character. Sometimes they do something ill-advised prior to a deployment, like tie one on and get arrested for Driving Under the Influence. Or maybe they injure themselves doing something out of their routine, like bungee jumping, or taking a mountain hike up a trail for advanced hikers, when they have never hiked beyond a road march.

And sometimes, they let circumstances support who they already are. Maybe a coward. Maybe disillusioned. Maybe a sociopath. Maybe they are simply someone that should not be among us.

When you're a military police officer, you experience the ebb and flow of raw emotion that consumes the base you are working. You get a front row seat to some of the most spectacularly poor judgment that any one person can exhibit. But with that comes the review of it all. The sadness and despair that a person can bring to their loved ones. The disgrace they bring to their peers, and their command.

But what if it all goes unanswered? What if in that moment, the chain of command simply cannot accept another solider lost prior to deployment? What if that soldier is highly regarded because they score on the PT test? What if that soldier represents the last soldier to maintain unit readiness? What happens when the loss of one means the unit falls apart, and the command faces loss of their own career or aspirations?

I was a young man at the age of 20, like we all were. I rode my ideals like a chopper heading down a sunny interstate. And my can-do attitude was impossible to shake. I'd been to some wild domestic violence calls, but none like the one I was about to experience.

The call came out of a physical assault taking place in a neighborhood on this base that had the reputation of domestic violence. It was a widely known fact among MP's here that this area just seemed to attract men and women who did more fighting than loving, and because it was norm, we were immune to what that actually meant.

My partner and I went to the call, the same as we would any assault; lights, sirens, a healthy dose of gas pedal, and disregard for all other things flashing along our windows as we make our way to the call.

We stop our car one house away, which is too close anyway, but we're brave men under the legal age to drink, carrying a batman belt.

To the house we march, slowing down as we approach edges of parked cars in the road, pausing at the middle of cars, hoping to hear noise that can help substantiate the complaint, and tell us how immediate we are needed.

We reach the far end of the house, a pair of windows, with the blinds down, but indoor light is peering through the blinds. We can hear a woman crying. At face value, one might write it off as the result of a strongly worded argument.

Just as we begin to make our way to the front door, a neighbor comes off their porch in the dark and shouts "He never stops with the hitting and shouting. You better do something about that! No way his Sergeant is going to let that go on!"

Thanks for announcing our presence sir, I think to myself. The front door opens, and the female who was crying looks at us and starts to cry harder. She has a distinct bruise on her right cheek bone, that appears to be the size of a half dollar that is forming and starting to show color. Terrific.

My partner asks her to step down from the doorway and onto the walkway. She shuts the door, takes a breath, looks at us again, and turns her face down and begins crying more.

177

"Hey, we're here now, and it's ok." I say in the calmest tone I can muster. I'm still a young man doing this job, and so I'm always keyed to the idea of threats looming. And while I want to assure this woman that the worst is over, I still have my eyes locked on that front door, because I don't know where the guy is that hit her, or what he has in his hands, or in his pockets, or in his bedroom, or in the kitchen, or at the ready by his feet. So many things to think about, not enough eyes to focus.

"He's gone." she blurts out. Finally, I can mentally peel myself away from what lies behind the door. She continued, "He left in his truck to his girlfriend's house. He said he'd have a story to counter mine when the MP's came."

Oh nice. Good to know we're concerned about our reputation among all this. I wouldn't want us to lose sight of the big picture. I guess the whole married with a girlfriend part is not of concern either.

"Can you tell me what happened?" I ask slowly.

"He hit me because I called his girlfriend in front of him. He thought I didn't know, and I put her on speaker, and as soon as he heard her, he hit me. Then he left."

"Has he hit you before?" I ask. At this point, my partner is motioning to me that we need to clear the house, and he's right.

"No, this is the first time. He's had problems with other women in the past. Not like this though." she said.

"Ma'am, is there anyone else in the house?" I ask.

"Just my daughter. She's four. She's asleep in her room." she says.

"Stay here, and we'll be right back." My partner calls on the radio that we're entering the home to clear it, and our patrol supervisor arrives just as we setup at the door.

I ask him to stay with the victim, and we go in, calling out for anyone in the house to walk towards us with their hands in the air. We clear the living room quickly, and then the kitchen. We make our way down the hallway, and find the daughter asleep. We clear her room, and she wakes up looking startled and scared.
"Hey, it's ok, your mom just wants us to check for monsters, we haven't found any yet. We'll be right back, ok?" I said.

"My daddy is mean; I hope you stop him." she said.

Clearly my anecdotal child-speak is useless here. She's already grown up enough to know the situation. We finish the job, and I knock on the girl's door.

"Are you ready to come out, we have to leave the house now." I say, my partner starts filing back out to the living room, making sure we didn't miss something out of place.

"Yea, I already got my backpack on." she says. A sure sign she's been through this before.

We walk out and she runs to her mother, who's trying to hold back tears as she smiles at the sight of her child.

"Ma'am, if you'd like we can escort you to the hospital, or we can drive you there to have the bruise looked at." my partner said.

"It's not necessary, honestly. I just want to go back into the house and go to bed." she said.

"Well, we have to get a statement from you about what happened tonight, and it's best if we do that at the station." he responded.

She drives herself to the station, and we take a report on the incident. Before she leaves, her husband, a large-framed man who probably is not at an acceptable weight for military standards, is brought in by another MP. You wouldn't label him fat, he's built more like a defensive tackle than a soldier. The MP that brought him in put two and two together when the truck came speeding by him a few minutes after the call came out, only a few blocks from the

180

house, and he admitted guilt on the ensuing traffic stop.

As we complete the statement, and escort the victim back out of the interview room to the lobby, her husband makes a plea to her from the bench he is now handcuffed to, saying it was an accident and he was sorry.

My partner and I parted ways with her after walking back to her car, and we proceeded to head for the basement of the station to type up our report. As we submitted our reports, the platoon sergeant came with the soldier's team leader, to pick up their shining example of catastrophe. Our patrol supervisor asked us to be present to answer questions before handing over the soldier.

The platoon sergeant never asked us the time, much less what his soldier had done. The team leader asked if the soldier would be subject to a criminal prosecution. "Only if your chain of command formalizes a complaint to the JAG Office." our patrol supervisor said.

"Ok, thanks." the team leader said, and with that the soldier was handed off. Considering the lack of questions, and the history of domestic violence on the base, my first thought was that the soldier would wind up running behind whatever vehicle the two sergeants came in, and then he would stay in the barracks for some time, never to be heard from again.

The next night, less than 24 hours later, another call for domestic assault at the same house. My partner and I were on, and assigned to the same sector, so just like any other call, we carried out our normal response, and arrived at the home. This time we showed up just as the soldier was intending to leave. As soon as he saw us, he tried starting his truck, and my partner and I ran to the driver's side, at which time the soldier put his hands up and we opened the door, and placed him in handcuffs.

The wife was leaning against a car down the street, and a neighbor was pressing a bag of ice against her right eye. "He did it again. You guys have to lock him up, he's not going to stop." the neighbor said to me.

"I'll take over the bag, why don't head back to your home." I said. The neighbor walked off, decidedly disgusted.

"How did he leave the barracks? Wasn't he being watched?" the wife asked me. "His unit is supposed to." I added, "but I venture to guess this time is going to change whatever they were doing. How bad does it hurt?" I asked. "I can't open it, every time I try, it burns." she said.

My partner and I drive her to the hospital, and they take a couple hours to treat her eye wound. I stay at the hospital with the victim, and she tells me about her marriage, and she expresses the failure she feels, and I can't stop feeling affected by the story.

"It wasn't like this in the beginning. I heard about his yelling, and his over the top emotion, but never did I hear about hitting." she said, while finally resting in a hospital bed.

It's a little surreal seeing a victim of recent trauma lying in a hospital bed. The scene doesn't feel much different than what it's like sitting with a dead person, except for the moments of conversation. That's when it becomes like life again.

"It shouldn't be doing this. His unit should have been watching. They're supposed to put them on barracks restriction. They're supposed to be watching him." I said.

"Well they don't. He's well regarded at his unit, so they don't care. Maybe if he didn't have the respect they'd care. But they don't, and I'm just in the way to them." she responded sharp.

"Don't say that. They can't let a soldier beat up his wife multiple times; it's their duty to keep you safe, too." I said.

"My mother is coming in three days, I'm already packing my belongings, and as soon as we can, I'm leaving for home. I'll be safe then." she said.

"You're safe here. This had to be a mistake, they wouldn't let him assault you without repercussions. They have a standard to uphold. I promise you, they cannot allow him to continue like this." I said.

She stayed silent after this, and when the hospital said she could leave, I called for a ride back to the station, and asked if she needed a ride home. She declined, a friend was coming, and while she didn't say it, I got the feeling she was sick of seeing me. I couldn't blame her.

I had the next two days off, which was probably well-timed. While I was off, the soldier managed to get away from his unit two days in a row. The fourth time, the MPs on duty were waiting near the house, saw his truck, stopped him, and placed him under arrest for violating the local base law, since he had been ordered to stay away from the house. This is an administrative charge, and in this case, should have led to Article 15 hearings for each incident, which should have then sparked a potential Court Martial. If I told you that happened, I'd be lying.

My next day on, I was supposed to work my regular assignment, which was at the station desk. But I asked a peer to cover my shift, and I went back on the road. I didn't want a day five to happen.

I stopped by the soldier's unit, and checked in with the staff duty office. He was shown as checked into his barracks room, and the soldier on duty had completed 15 minute checks of him since 5:15 PM that day, all indicating he was in his room.

I decided to check on him myself, maybe more proactive than my leadership would have wanted, but not out of line. I knocked on his door.

"Oh, how can I help you MP?" he asked, in a friendly, and sarcastic manner. "Just wanted to make sure we're going to stay in our room until further notice. We don't want any more assaults." I said. "It's really not like that, I know I should be acting better. I just want to talk about our relationship, but she acts like it's over and then..." he said.

"Whatever you feel, it's not worth your career. Don't go over there again until you are told otherwise." I interrupted.

Those words he said, are the words of an abuser who will never change. I knew it then just as well as I know it now. The difference is, I tried to reason with him, thinking that if I responded nicely, I might get the result I desired. Gaining voluntary compliance from anyone can be a tricky game.

I went out onto shift and handled a few minor calls. Luckily, I wasn't assigned to a sector, I was out in a car waiting this night, waiting for a call I didn't want to take.

Around 11:45 PM, the radio cracked off, "All units, we have a report of domestic assault…." Damn it!

I flew down the road and swooped into the neighborhood. Another unit got there before I did and already had him in custody. "Idiot!" That was all I could think as I began marching into the yard looking for her. In retrospect, maybe I was calling myself one more so than I was calling him one. I would gather it applied equally on both counts.

My supervisor for the night showed up and told me to help deal with the solider at the station, since I knew the history well. I followed the other officer to the station, and we began processing his arrest quickly, wanting to make sure we had everything done long before his command came to pick him up.

He tried explaining to me why he did it. I didn't take the interview, but I sat with the other MP writing the statement form while I prepared the rights advisement and release form. This was the first time I saw a Desk Sergeant require brigade leadership to pick up a soldier. When the company and battalion leadership came, the Sergeant stood his ground fantastically and told them that they can wait in the lobby until the brigade leadership shows up. That took two hours, but when they came, the Sergeant handed the Colonel the paperwork and told him that his leadership has failed to control a solider, who has assaulted his own wife five days in a row.

The temperature in the room changed, and the Colonel said to bring the soldier out, and when we did the first thing I heard was "BEAR CRAWL!" And with that, the soldier left the building on his hands and feet, and continued down the walkway into the street, and the Colonel all the while was tearing into his leadership group. While it was a poetic scene, I have my doubts as to what good it did.

I asked my supervisor if I could go up to the hospital. He permitted me to, but told me it was no use getting a statement. When I got there, I could see why. She was in an ER bed, waiting for a room upstairs. She was unconscious, and had a respiratory tube in her mouth. She was so lifeless. I could feel my heart sink into my stomach. Her mother was in the room, and saw me at the door.

"Oh, you're here for her statement, like the others, right?" she asked. "No ma'am, I just wanted to see how she was doing. I can see this isn't a good time. I'm sorry." I trailed to a whisper to the end of statement.

"Yea, not a good time. How about the yesterday, or the day before that, or the day before that, oh hell, Monday? Was that a good time? Did you get what you needed then? I sure hope so, because at this rate, my daughter is going to be brain dead, and you'll all look really great coming around asking for her statement and she'll barely be able to say hello." she yelled.

I could hear the tears and the agony in her voice. "I'm really sorry ma'am, I promise I didn't want this..." she interrupted me. "Oh, a promise? One of you promised her this couldn't happen again, and then it happened three days in a row after that. Now you're promising what you didn't want? What about my daughter?! What about her promise, to be alive, to be a mother, to be happy?!? Have any promises for that?" She started crying, and by this time medical staff started showing up.

"I'm really sorry ma'am." I said, before leaving like the building was falling down around me. I sat in my patrol car, feeling like I had just been punched over every part of my core. My arms were heavy like cinder blocks. I drove to an empty parking lot and sat for a while. Another MP from another unit drove up next to me, I didn't know him well.

"Tough call, Private?" he referenced my rank. "Yea." I managed to say with half a slur. "They come and they go. Can't let it beat you down. The next one, you may actually get to stop them. But don't ever think you can stop them all. This job is mostly about picking up the pieces after everything has already happened." he said confidently.

I sat silently. I couldn't think of a way to respond. Not that he wasn't right, I just was lost. We often think of the world we live in as being safe. And especially here, where we experience a level of safety in everyday life that much of the rest of the world prays for.

But, I can tell you for sure, I can't promise you'll always be safe. And I can't promise you that everything works the way it's supposed to. Many of the things that keep us safe are dependent on people who care to do the task. And when they fail, the rest of us fail with them. I wish I could tell you that all things end well eventually, but we both have had enough experience in this world to know better. There's not a day that goes by that I don't feel regret. But I know that I did everything my job allowed me to do. And the days I was on patrol, were not even on my regular schedule. But I never can shake how devolved this call became. It sticks in my head like a tension headache that won't respond to Excedrin. It haunts me, and has caused me so many sleepless nights. The feeling of failure, the hopelessness of her mother, how the soldier's wife spoke to me in a way that suggested she already knew where this was going, and how empty my words came off to her.

There are just some promises we can't keep.

NICHOLAS LIST
United States Army

"What the fuck is wrong with you, dipshit!?"

That's what the black silhouette of my Bradley commander screamed at me as he stood on the rim of our track's driver's hatch. It was almost midnight and despite being sleep deprived, I could feel that chill creep into my stomach when I know I messed up. Yeah, I screwed up big time. You know how I know I fucked up? Because the front of the hull of our $3 million Bradley was now resting on a concrete berm.

That's right, my first night driving in an actual table VII gunnery, and I rammed a very expensive armored fighting vehicle I don't own into an object that really doesn't give a shit how heavy or how much horse power our track has. On our BC's command, *"Driver up!"*, I was to pull the track up just far enough forward in our defensive position for the gunner to fire his engagement. After the engagement, he was to say, *"Cease fire, driver back!"*, and I would reverse our track back to a position where only our Bradley's periscopes would be visible.

There would be no "cease fire, driver back" on this engagement, because I left my foot on the accelerator too damn long. At that moment, I began to try to put a positive spin in my brain about the circumstances of my shitty driving. The Bradley would be okay. A hit like that on a track didn't cause any real damage, other than some scratched paint. This was not the gunnery table that counted for qualification, so our crew would have another chance. This was not only my first time driving in a gunnery; it was also the night portion so that's got to count for something... right? It did count for something. It's just that it counted for everyone that couldn't help me with what was going to happen next.

I wasn't supposed to be driving that night. I was a dismount/loader for another Bradley and not technically on that crew. It was a last-minute decision to replace the driver that I was way too eager to jump on. You see, I had been in the Army for a little under a year and had already discovered that being on a firing crew made you a rock star. They were impervious to the various shitty tasks that were forced on uninitiated privates. A Bradley crewman was respected for doing the actual warfighting. I always dreamed of being one of the guys rocking the CVC (combat vehicle crewman) coveralls that made you look like a Wal-Mart fighter pilot.

Eventually after receiving the Staff Sergeant's colorfully constructive criticism under the "needs improvement" blank of my counseling session, our Bradley commander returned to his commander's hatch and proceeded to berate me over the vehicle's intercom. This wouldn't have been such a big deal if he wasn't still transmitting to the range tower at the time. We in the business like to call that "Hot miking". An ass chewing for the ages, with an audience. I wonder if they ever saved that tape?

Despite still feeling shitty about the current state of things, I had to laugh at the sound of our gunner pulling the BC's CVC helmet cable to keep him from dropping more F-bombs on the net. If I had known the tight rope that our gunner walked on when dealing with my newly appointed squad leader, I may not have been so quick to laugh. As a matter of fact, our gunner pulling the cable to keep our squad leader from doing something that would fuck him over would become a reoccurring theme that I would eventually have to adapt to.

I felt like there was no way to renew my squad leader's confidence in me. When we got back from the field, I was hoping, praying my fuck up would land me in another squad, and I didn't care how many crappy details I had to endure. Shit, my first field problem my Platoon Sergeant left me at the Battery TOC (Tactical Operation Center) was to pull KP (Kitchen Police). Then he pretty much forgot I was there for almost 2 weeks. He actually apologized when he finally brought me back to the platoon, but I thought it was a pretty sweet deal. Three hot meals, heated tents, I got a cot to sleep on, and all I had to do was scrap grits out of a pan!

Well there would be a steady supply of misery from my squad leader, but not like my previous one, who actually employed healthy negative reinforcement to turn us into better soldiers. His method was mostly to assign me to any tasks that would keep me out of his hair and out of being seen in any positive situation. At the time, I convinced myself I deserved this from him; but I really had no idea what was going on with him. He barely showed up for formations, and when he did, it was specifically to do something to mess with me. Turning me over to whoever needed bodies for any garbage task he could find. Changing my assigned weapon to a M249 just on the basis it was heavier. (Jokes on him, easiest weapon to qualify expert on ever!)

All that shit really didn't hurt. What did hurt was getting treated like I was a burden. I dealt with this in a self-destructive way—by drinking. It's a common coping mechanism, but not the best response. I think this goes without saying, but in the military, there is an entire culture of disillusioned junior enlisted soldiers who take this as an acceptable medium to deal with work-related stress. It becomes the norm, easier than talking about your feelings, and cheaper than counseling, especially when said counseling could endanger your security clearance.

On a Thursday morning, as I lined up in formation, I noticed my squad leader was missing yet again. I didn't mind, another day without him "motivating" me wouldn't hurt. Our gunner seemed less calm about this, as he had been working in the squad leader's capacity for nearly 8 months, about the time he started missing formations routinely. When our platoon sergeant asked my gunner to report where his staff sergeant was, his reply was simply a grimace and a shake of the head. Our gunner, a Specialist with a good reputation for watching out for his squad, even when it didn't deserve it, finally had no excuses left to give.

Our Platoon Sergeant received the rest of the platoon's report and told our squad leaders to take charge, conduct inspection, and begin training. I saw him head to his POV (Privately Operated Vehicle) and drive off. I knew where he was going. Our gunner did, too, and he looked nervous about it.

At the end of day, while we were moving into our close of business formation behind our S&A (Supply and Admin) building, I saw my squad leader with my platoon sergeant, first sergeant, battery commander, and an MP (Military Police). Because the situation was awkward for all involved, we were quickly dismissed from formation and told to go home, but we all saw what was up.

Later, my gunner told me what our platoon sergeant saw when he got to our squad leader's home. His quarters were in disarray, which was disturbing considering he shared the residence with his step-children. On his lovely glass coffee table, there was a suspicious powdery, white substance, which upon further testing, would reveal its chemical composition to be methamphetamine.

After that, I never saw that staff sergeant again. I heard he got assigned to the headquarters troop while they worked out the details of his "transition." Apparently, the length of his absence, combined with the substance abuse, led to some unique disciplinary circumstances.

After feeling vindicated for a whopping 30 seconds, I was left in a very confusing state. I still felt like I was a dumbass, regardless of what ever situation my previous squad leader was going through. Our gunner, God bless him, treated me akin to something like an abused spouse. He seemed like he felt genuinely guilty about what happened to me. I could probably be more pissed at the fact that my "leadership" was a guy who preferred controlled substances over fulfilling his obligation to the service he took an oath for, but honestly, I learned a valuable lesson through that experience about how the Army perceives subordinates: Perform well, get away with more.

Not long after his departure, I was afforded the opportunity to perform well. Our unit had a waiver to promote a specialist, but due to a soldier that had been initially selected for this position getting himself into a disciplinary issue, the 4 platoons of the battery were pining to get one of their boys in that slot. With all the candidates having roughly the same professional performance, the leadership decided a board would be the best option. For those who have not experienced in Army promotion policies, a board is a formal means to determine suitability for a candidate by interviewing him/her in front of his unit's staff leadership.

This interview is not like one you would normally get for a job. There is a lot of pomp behind it that I could probably write a thesis on if given the opportunity. You're supposed to sit at the position of *attention* from which the president of the board will tell you to *relax*. The unwritten rule is that you are never to relax. You are to look and act as if you absolutely know what you are doing even if you don't. This is a task military leadership has mastered over the years.

I surprised a lot of people when I did so well at the board. I mostly surprised myself, just when I was beginning to think my label of *shit bag* was an accurate description. My platoon sergeant was very pleased, and I was thinking things were looking up. I had shown that I was not completely useless, and that if given an opportunity I can keep it together. Despite that, I still had issues with my professional state. I had a brief alcohol-related incident that kept me from accepting orders that I received for Korea. It was nothing serious, I hurt no one nor damaged property. I was admitted to the post hospital for mild hypothermia. The first Sergeant even said "List, this shit is funnier than anything. You know I got to punish you right?" He put my rank on suspension, which means they can take my rank for whatever reason. You would think that would be enough to keep me from drinking.

For obvious reasons, our military became a very different organization after 9/11. I remember that day well. I had seen what was going to be an otherwise standard day in the army, turn into one of the most surreal things a 19-year-old could experience. One of the things that happened was that with installation locked down, we were instantly short on people to guard the post. This led to us being in a state of bizarre cross-assignment that separated us from our units almost constantly. I brought my drinking to a halt, that is until the end of the year. At that point, the threat condition dropped and we were back to our old training schedule. So, I went back to my old drinking schedule, which was pretty much any down time I had.

While I was seen by most of the platoon as competent, there was one Squad Leader who has his doubts. While looking back at this I could understand his reasons. I was a drunk; a competent one, but still a drunk. I had fulfilled several roles in the months after 9/11. In that time, I had advanced to a gunner slot, but had not officially qualified on a crew. I was in a better place, but not actually feeling better. If only I knew what fate had in store for me, I would have made more of an effort to show up sober.

On a cold Thursday morning in January, I was at our battery S&A (Supply and Administration area) for formation. I was hungover, as we were having a going away party for one of our guys the night before. That's no excuse, but I felt like I could use some help looking like less of an asshole at that point. That one squad leader I mentioned previously who had his doubts about me was ready to take this transgression further. Our third squad leader told me he was *this* close to calling the MP's, but one Sergeant Andrew Pokorny talked to him. Sergeant Pokorny was my new squad leader. He had just got to his unit to find his gunner, his second in command of the Bradley, hungover. I remember when he called me over to speak alone. The 29-year-old looked at me with the eyes that your dad gives you when he's very disappointed with you and said, "List, you know that the first squad leader was about to call the MP's on you right?"

I grimaced and replied, "Yes." Pokorny said, "Well, I told him not to do that. I asked him if you know what you're doing on the job, and he thinks you do. I'm going to give you a chance, because I'm new to this job, and I need someone to get me up to speed. Don't ever show up like this again, or else I'll deal with you." I felt relieved and ashamed and the same time. I said, "Yes Sergeant."

This was something different. He didn't even know me. If anything, I screwed him over on his first day by being jacked up. No one had ever done something like that for me before. I was determined to show him he made the right decision. He saved me, so I was going to do the best I could for him.

It's not an overstatement to say Sergeant Andrew Pokorny is the kind of man that made me proud to be a soldier. He was in the battle of Mogadishu and placed heavy emphasis in riflemen skills. He would always look out for our wellbeing, not just professionally, but personally. He really believed that good leadership is owed to the soldier, and that we were all important. He was sincere to the point that it would hurt you to let him down.

We were about to start our training cycle; a gunnery and a maneuver exercise (Wargames). Our platoon was to load our Bradleys with the necessary inventory for the field. By this time, I already had a really good idea how to prepare for it. So much so that Sergeant Pokorny asked me "Well, what do I do?"

I simply replied, "For now, just enjoy the ride Sergeant!"

Our time in the field was a defining moment for both of us. We were a new crew, untested as an actual cohesive unit.

During the gunnery, we earned a *Superior* rating which was not bad for a new crew. The highlight of which was when we shot down the RCMAT (Remote Control Moving Aerial Target). There wasn't much left but one of the guys from the platoon snagged the tail before it burned to a crisp. I was sure to bring it back with me.

During the exercise in the Pinion Canyon Maneuver area, we practiced some dismounted tactics that turned to an impromptu 13-mile force march and ended with us scaling a hundred foot, dried up waterfall. I remember at mile ten we used up all our water. The gunner off another track had one last canteen but didn't break it out because it was still a little soapy from when his wife cleaned it. Well that was one of the best damn drinks of water we had in our lives. We sat at the bottom of a steep ravine. Even though our radio batteries were almost dead, and we couldn't reach anyone in the unit, we felt good, assured and confident. It was one of the moments I felt like I loved the army.

We eventually linked back up with the platoon and continued the exercise with the rest of the 3rd ACR. The rest of it seemed almost boring by comparison, but we still did the job. After three weeks of sucking diesel fumes, we were mounting our Bradleys back on a train to return to Ft. Carson. SSG Pokorny was rechecking the chains securing our track to the car, when he lost his grip on the breaker bar and came flying off the train. He fell fifteen feet, and unbeknownst to me at the time, I was right under him. I broke his fall without even being aware of it. He swore I saved his life. I just felt like I was in the right place at the right time.

I came up for reenlistment, and decided to get Germany in my contract since everyone who came from there raved about it. Very few things in the Army are as advertised, but Germany was the exception. Despite the ancient equipment (I think one Bradley's serial number was 000025), Alpha Battery 4th battalion 3rd regiment 1st ID was a disciplined, high standards unit.

While out at a bar in downtown Kitzigen, I heard that we had some new soldiers from my old unit come in. Low and behold, Barrett, a guy from my platoon at Carson was one. I hadn't heard much from those guys since they had Deployed to Iraq in 2003. I asked him how Sgt. Pokorny was. The look he gave me said it all. I had to hear him say it though. I really wish I hadn't. I don't remember the last time I cried like that. Staff Sergeant Andrew R. Pokorny was killed in a vehicle rollover on June 13, 2003. Our unit was set to deploy soon after, and I found myself vowing to do him proud in Iraq, if only to dull the pain of not being there to save him.

When we finally deployed, it was disorienting on the way to Iraq from Kuwait. Our FOB (Forward Operating Base) was next to the Tigris in a palace complex surrounded by a wall and reinforced with Hesco barriers. We got there at about midnight. I remember our leadership saying we really had nothing else to do but wait for the rest of our unit since 4th Infantry Division was still pulling force protection. Exhausted from the trip, I rolled out my PT mat and sleeping bag on the cool marble floor of the semi-intact palace. It was one of the best night's sleep I ever had despite being stressed about being there. I found myself thinking about Sergeant Pokorny a lot from then on out. I tried hard to not blame myself for him dying in that place a year before I got there, but it was damn hard not to. I even remember the reenlistment NCO saying, "Well, you could re-enlist to stay here with us."

Those words tortured me for a long time and still kind of do. I've had a lot of "what ifs" since then. It helped when I thought about what I would say to him now that I can't. I'd want to tell him that what he taught me directly contributed to my survival. I wanted to tell him that even though he's not with me, he still keeps me alive. That my son who bears his name, the opportunity to be with the woman I love, and all the best parts of my life that I have are thanks to him. I would tell him I hope he knows I love him even if I didn't always admit it. I would tell him that I hope he will haunt me for the rest of days.

REBECCA BROWN
United States Marines

If you've ever watched a pair of jeans slowly frazzle and wear out along the hem around the bottom of your shoe, you know the part that scrapes the ground when you walk if your jeans are too long...then you know what my life was like watching my parents fall apart through my high school years. I played basketball during the early 90's at a new school my junior and senior year and the transition was hard. It was even harder with parents that were drifting apart kind of like seaweed in the break of a wave.

By 1996, I was 22 years old preparing for college graduation with a Bachelor's in sociology, had a boyfriend that was older and pretty cool and I was an All-American basketball player who had the whole world by the tail but I didn't have a job and didn't have a home to go to once I graduated. I really didn't know what to do with my life.

Once my parents split I was given a choice; at the time, I didn't think I chose right nevertheless, I suppose maybe I did. Either way, the boyfriend was a four-year veteran Marine Corps grunts. He served on active duty during Desert Storm and tales of his tour read like an old war novel or silver screen movie. I knew all his buddies, even though I'd never met a single one, through his photo albums and outlandish, romanticized stories over gallons of beer.

One day I found myself on the blacktop courts of southwest Georgia playing streetball. I was the only female. I looked over at the end of the court and I saw the ugliest mother fucker I've ever seen. I recognized the uniform straight away and it was sharp but he was one ugly mother fucker. He was covered in tattoos on every piece of skin from his ears to his fingertips and I thought is that really what Marines look like?! No way, I thought. I was dating a Marine and I knew not all Marines looked like this thug but here he was, somehow introducing himself to me. I still don't know why I shook his hand that day. I figured since I'd already spent four years in an institution where there were three hots and a cot, why listen to what the man had to say about another one. I couldn't stay where as was and I sure as hell couldn't go home.

I recall talking to my parents before I signed up; I remember my Daddy telling me 'you're going to be a college grad, you're going to be an officer. You need to go officer so you can have a desk job'.

I told him I wanted to be enlisted like he was so that I could learn from the bottom up how to lead Marines. I was smart enough to know that I couldn't lead Marines if I didn't know how to take orders. I didn't tell my Daddy until after the deed was done. Upon returning from MEPS, sitting in the recruiter's office, I called him very excited and proud. As he answered, his first words were 'tell me that you chose officer'. The look on the recruiter's face as I held the phone away from my ear was priceless. I'm pretty sure he thought he was gonna get slaughtered.

Over the next few months' lots of things happened. I broke the news to my boyfriend, who was not as enthusiastic as I was, that I had joined his beloved Marine Corps. We ran into some rough spots while my delayed entry period got longer than planned. We ended up splitting because he said he didn't want a woman who would go through what he had to go through.

Over the next 6 months while I was in the delayed entry program, I learned what it meant to want to be a Marine. I learned because even though I thought I was a big-name athlete (turns out I was just a big fish in a small pond) and that I could handle the Corps, I did not have what it took to be a Marine. I ran daily; I did the daily 13; my Daddy even built a 7-foot wall in our backyard because during DEP training I was unable to clear the wall in the obstacle course. By the end of that six months, I had figured out how to do it. You might call that cheating but I called it groundwork. I also made life-long friends who still have my back today.

My recruiter asked me what I wanted to do in the Corps (like I really had a snowball's chance in hell of getting what I wanted but it was his job to make me think I would) so the response of 'I have no idea but I don't want to sit behind a fucking desk' made him riot with laughter.

"You can drive a truck or you can be a mechanic and that's about it because you're a woman" he roared in between bursts of belly laughs.

I looked at him with condescension, "Well what does it take to be a mechanic?"

"You have to have a high enough ASVAB score, if you do, you can pretty much choose the type of job you want."

After that meeting I called home, "Daddy, I need to be a mechanic so teach me what you know!" He had been a jet crew chief mechanic in the Air Force during Vietnam, so he knew what it would take for me to get the job I wanted. For the next three months, we sat at the kitchen table and studied for the ASVAB. He taught me everything he knew in the mechanics field in a crash, make you're freaking head spin, course but I had to be a mechanic. No way was I going to sit behind a desk as a woman.

At the end of boot camp - I'm not even going to talk about boot camp, its common knowledge - I went through the Crucible - designed in 1996 - to emphasize the importance of teamwork in overcoming adversity, it is a rigorous 54-hour field training exercise demanding the application of everything a us Marine recruit has learned until that point in recruit training and includes a total of 48 miles of marching. It simulates typical combat situations with strenuous testing, hardship, and

deprivation of food and sleep. I graduated March 7,
1997.

Prior to 1997, after graduation, all female Marines
went on leave and went right back to Parris Island
for a few weeks of training, then to MOS school and
onto the fleet. Because someone decided that the
statement, "Every Marine is a Rifleman" should
extend to females, I was in the first female platoon
to go Camp Geiger for Marine Corps Combat
Training or MCT, with males.

A mock war pitted four platoons 3 males and 1
female platoons to simulate what had been learned
since stepping on the yellow footprints. Since I am
6' 3", I was assigned as the M240G, which I
affectionately named Aaron. I was assigned an A
gunner, Pvt. Foss, who carried the bipod and
ammunition, since Aaron weighed in at a hefty 25
lbs. I slept with him, ate with him, and humped with
him. Damn he was heavy. It felt good though. I felt
a purpose. I felt like a Marine.

During one of our evening patrols, we engaged our
enemy in a simulated firefight. As we flanked the
enemy, we were able to capture a POW. My sergeant
ordered me to search the prisoner. This is when the
fun began; I took the prisoner by his wrist, slammed
him against a pine tree, patted him down, threw his
scrawny ass to the ground with foot to the back of
his knee and face planted him into the cold mud,
man that shit was fun. It was all fun because there

were no live rounds, no fear, no blood, no guts; all glory.

My sergeant was a large, crazy mother, kinda like BA from the old TV show A Team and I'm certain he had PTSD. That mother fuckers' chest was so big a flak jacket wouldn't close around him. Aaron made me a bad bitch like Animal Mother and I'm confident the sergeant thought so, too. One day during a firefight, ceasefire was called and while in our positions, we were told to allow the enemy squad to walkthrough (for training purposes).

Scrawny, dirty kids, just like us. Tired, nasty and hungry, slinking their way through our fighting positions like snakes. Each one of them had smirks, on their mud caked faces, as they were certain they'd whipped the females. I maintained eye contact with my sergeant, as he sat on a downed pine tree about 50 yards away. Prior to the ceasefire, I had crawled out of my foxhole and began to lay down fire with the M240G between my legs as I crouched beside a tree. I watched and waited for him to give me the well-known 'I'm watching you, you're watching me', knowing he had the same idea: "BROWN" he roared, "OPEN FIRE". I pulled the trigger and wasted those fuckers!

Their Sergeant was pretty pissed but all's fair in Love and War.

In the end, the commanding officer of the whole thing said female platoon won the war. Looking back, it was probably because he was trying to be PC or some BS. I'm pretty sure we did win because we all were legendary badasses in our own minds. I still keep in touch with most of them, via social media. We're still pretty much badasses in our own way.

I could have told you all about my time in the fleet but you hear enough of that stuff. I will say, unless you are a Woman Marine, WM, you just don't know how tough it can get. Yeah, I get it, we asked for it because we joined a man's world, trying to do manly things but really, it's not about trying to be a man or do manly things.

If I can help you understand, to most of us, it's about serving our country. About having a sense of honor, pride, duty and respect for where we came from and where we're going. Being a WM, it's tricky, you know, to be in a man's world. The balance isn't easy but most of the time, all we want to do is our job and protect our country and our way of life. Most of us don't ask for much, we go with the flow. It's not that too much is expected of us; sometimes it's that not enough is expected. Or that the wrong thing is expected of us. Most of us still want to be a woman but we have a desire to be more, so we join the Marines.

We're getting to the point where you might wonder: do I think that women belong in combat? Now, I'm not a combat veteran but that doesn't change my opinion of women fighting. I was in that group of female firsts but I just don't see that women belong in combat. There are women who are mentally strong; who can handle seeing slaughter, violence, rape, and torture. And, there are women able to handle the rigors that come along with the physical side of being in combat, no doubt. But does that mean that they belong in a combat unit? Sure, it's a matter of fact that if a woman is sent to a combat zone situation, she's likely going to have to react in a combative nature. However, if and when you put that woman in with a group of men, it changes the whole makeup of the fire team, the squad, the platoon, the company, the battalion. You say, well make an all-female unit. I'm against that as well. For most men, it's his emotional need to protect a woman. I believe it is the law of nature and in a situation where there is danger, I feel it is more likely a man would protect a woman than he would another man. You can read all the studies by Harvard, Yale or anyone else that you want but this is my opinion. I've seen hardcore Marines protect a woman over their fellow male Marine when the shit hit the fan. I will tell you this: because of a few good men I am here today. Because they stood up for me during times when I could not stand up for myself.

Taking nothing away from my Corps sisters, my guy friends are my big brothers and I will never forget how they chose to protect their sister during an internal combat situation. For that I'm eternally grateful.

Semper Fi

SCOTT MEEHAN
United States Army

Fort Benning, Georgia
August 1980

Sweat dripped down my face like a waterfall in the Amazon jungle, thanks to the hundred-degree heat. Topped off with the brutal Georgian humidity, our drenched T-shirts stuck to our bodies like hot glue. This was just a small price to pay for the privilege of becoming a US Army paratrooper.

The cadre marched more than one hundred of us, in several different groups, to the outdoor overhead showers for a cool-down session. There, we would lie down on a hot concrete slab, much like a wide driveway, and then roll across the cement like bowling balls in our olive drab pants and sweat-stained white T-shirts. Several overhead pipes, evenly spaced in rows, sprayed showers of water down upon us, soaking our bodies, and what was once our previously inspected, highly spit-shined boots.

Ah, what a relief the cool spray of water was to our physical need for hydration. However, the moment of pleasure ended too quickly. Little time passed before our bodies absorbed the liquid like a sponge, and the blazing sun zapped the moisture back away from us. Today, however, training was a priority, and the outdoor shower would have to wait for another hour or so.

During our first full week of training, we learned to exit from a door position by jumping out of a thirty-four-foot tower while being hooked up to a bungee cord. The cord slid down a long wire that extended to the far end of the field, where other soldiers waited to catch those who had just jumped.

Other drills focused us on keeping our feet together, evaluated by sliding down a T-bar and letting go when the cadre, affectionately called *black-hats*, told us to drop-fall to the ground quickly to administer push-ups.

They also analyzed our landing, ensuring that our feet were together, and we fell on the correct four points of contact.

Throughout the first week, no matter where I looked across the field, there were trainees scattered in every direction doing push-ups for one infraction or another, all under the gentle watch care of the black hat that stood over them.

Airborne School was an adventure that I hoped would play a large part in my attempt to become a man. Only four months prior to being in this sweat-hole, I had entered the army at Fort Leonard Wood, Missouri. Prior to that moment of enlistment, I had spent four years wandering throughout the United States, including a year at a small college, looking for the answer to what I should do with my life.

Everything seemed to end in disappointment or failure, all factors that led me to attempt to become one of America's elite fighting men.

Two weeks after the finish of ground zero, and four years after I first began searching for direction in my life, I was walking out the door of a C-141 jet aircraft...while in flight. I vividly recall the experience, the exhilarating memory of the event remaining clear to this day.

First were my emotions on the night before my first scheduled jump. I went for a walk until I spotted a log lying at the edge of some woods. Sitting down, and remembering a soldier at Fort Sam Houston, Texas, who was always lifting a small New Testament out of his shirt pocket during breaks, I reached for my little green issued Bible.

Opening its tiny pages, I flipped to the words, "Trust in the Lord with all your heart and don't lean on your own understanding. In all your ways acknowledge Him and He will direct your paths" (Proverbs 3:5–6). Those words were a sense of comfort to me that evening, and I was as ready as ever to jump from an aircraft while in flight.

The big day of my first jump began in a large open hangar with wooden tables attached side-by-side, room enough for all the jump-gear that a couple of hundred soon-to-be airborne soldiers would need. Once the process of suiting up was complete—a carefully executed partnership process—I stepped behind the soldier in front of me as we walked single file out onto the tarmac toward the three-awaiting aircraft. Several other lines of soldiers inched their way toward the lumbering birds as well.

Here we were, long lines of future paratroopers dressed in olive drab uniforms with a bright yellow static line running down our backs from the packed chute. As we headed to the open end of the aircraft, where ramps stretched out before us, the scene reminded me of exotic caterpillars crawling toward their predetermined destination. One by one the lines split apart toward one of the three designated planes, a C-130 and a C-123, both propeller planes, and a C-141 jetliner.

I was not sure how to react to the fact that I was in the line heading toward the jet. Then, methodically, each iron bird engulfed the prodding green and yellow line like a bird with a wide-open mouth swallowing a worm. I made my way up the ramp behind the others and then stumbled to the red-strapped jump seats situated along the skin of the aircraft and facing toward the middle. What made matters more complicated was the fact that there were also more jump seats placed at the center of the aircraft facing us. This uncomfortable squeeze forced bulkily packed soldiers to cramp together, face-to-face and knee-to-knee as we all made a desperate attempt to sit down like normal people. The word sardines came to mind.

Joining the army was not a planned event for me.

However, banging around the United States for four years after graduating high school and then spending a year at an expensive private college was not working for me. In fact, nothing seemed to be. My grades in college dictated that I needed to find some type of focus in my life. But what?

It was my dad who decided to help me along by visiting the marine recruiter on his own without my knowledge. Up for furlough from Ecuador, the former Baltimore County police officer and now missionary pilot had talked me into at least visiting and talking with a recruiter from each service branch. It did not take long for him to convince me that I probably did indeed need something drastic, like the military.

Coincidently, I had just completed reading a book by Robin Moore titled, *The Green Beret*, after some thought, I headed back to the army recruiter and asked the staff sergeant to tell me more about the Green Berets. My dad and mom had already departed back to Ecuador shortly after the holidays. The recruiter's sales pitch snagged me, completely as I pictured myself training and helping indigenous people in tribes and villages around the world to fight Communism and free the oppressed.

The Special Forces is just what I need! Before the ink was dry on the forms to sign my life away to Uncle Sam, I envisioned myself as one of the elite.

To get there, I would have to become accustomed to

jumping out of planes.

Both of my parents were shocked to discover what I had done. My mother was against me going into the military from the start. Nevertheless, despite my mother's resistance, the time came for me to leave, and I took the bus down to Miami and pledged to defend the Constitution against enemies, foreign and domestic. Next thing I knew, I was on a jet airliner flying to St. Louis in route to Fort Leonard Wood for basic training. Then, it was onward to Fort Benning, Georgia.

In just moments after being settled, the planes revved into action and lurched forward with a jerk, one after the other. Then, with little time to think too deeply about what we were prepared to do, the three planes were airborne with their contents packed with soon-to-be paratroopers. There was no time to get comfortable. Action began almost immediately with every shouted command. The first one came abruptly.

"Six minutes," the jumpmaster yelled while holding up five fingers on one hand and his thumb from the other!
"Six minutes," we all echoed back with a shout.

My mind kicked into gear: *Think quickly now; listen carefully!* Training mode set in, and I was on autopilot!
"Outboard personnel, stand up!" I could barely hear the screaming commands above the noise of the jet

engines.

Had it been six minutes already?

Those of us sitting with our backs toward the exterior of the aircraft stood up clumsily, bumping into the soldiers on either side of us in the process.

"Inboard personnel, stand up!"

To complicate matters, now those facing the exterior of the plane stood up, knocking into us and causing some to lose their footing. I held out my hand trying to grab anything to keep me from falling.

"Hook up!" the jumpmaster continued to yell.

After repeating this command, we all hooked our metal clasps attached to our yellow static lines to a cable running the length of the aircraft from front to back. Metallic clinking sounds could be heard above the droning of the jet engine.

"Check static line!"

After repeating the commands again, we all complied, making sure that there was no visual damage, such as frays or tears with the line running down the back of the trooper in front of us. Then we turned around to repeat the process with the ones behind us.

"Check equipment!"

I looked at myself to make sure that all fastening devices were intact and that nothing had come loose. Being separated from my parachute once I exited the aircraft...no!

"Sound off for equipment check!" The jumpmaster's commands were in rapid progression.

The last soldier facing the jumpmaster was the closest one to the front of the aircraft as we faced the rear. He slapped the soldier in front of him and yelled, "Okay!"

The domino effect of slapping the rear of the soldier in front of him and yelling, Okay, continued down the line until I felt the hard slap on my cheek, immediately prompting me to do likewise to the trooper in front of me.

"Okay!" I yelled with vigor.

Then the process continued until the last slap reached the soldier standing directly in front of the jumpmaster standing at the door. He looked the jumpmaster square in the eyes and yelled at the top of his lungs, "All okay, jumpmaster!"

Everything was by the book so far. The butterflies inside me flapped faster and faster.

"Two minutes!" The jumpmaster continued to yell. *We did all that in four minutes?*

The air was gushing in through the door as we stood

looking around, sweating and trying not to look scared to our peers.

"One minute!"

The tension increased. My heart beat faster. I swallowed hard.

"Thirty seconds!"
No time to change my mind now!

"Stand by!" The jumpmaster was positioning himself to aid those exiting the aircraft, or to make sure that they did leave out the door.

"Stand in the door!"

Then the jumpmaster firmly grabbed the static line from the first jumper while the jumper walked toward the open door of the jet plane. The light over the door was red. He stood frozen, waiting for the signal. The wind gushed through the open side door along with the jet engines making it difficult to hear.

The red light above the door turned green. "Go!"

The soldier in front of me began moving, and I found myself following like a robot, inching closer and closer to the open door. My mind was in the fast lane thinking of all the things I had trained to do in the past three weeks, leading up to this very moment.

Then, in seconds, before I knew it, the soldier in front of me vanished. It happened so fast. I looked into the eyes of the jumpmaster, less than a second, and handed him my static line, not wanting anything bad to happen. Then I put my head down, my hands over my reserve and began walking forty-five degrees toward the open door of the jet aircraft.

Whoosh! I'm a Nolan Ryan fastball! was my first thought. I immediately began my count, "One thousand, two thousand, threeeugh..." a tremendous jerk yanked me higher into the sky. I yelled like a spectator at a sporting event!
After quickly looking up to check my "can of peas" — the name the black hats used to jokingly refer to the canopy — I made sure that there were no tears or rips of any kind. Then I looked around for the other jumpers, making sure I was well clear of any flybys.

The song, *Sailing,* by Christopher Cross, came to mind since it was heard repeatedly on the jukebox during breaks. Another song was also popular during that time, but I did not want to think about that one from Queen, *Another One Bites the Dust.*

Then, the ground came rushing up toward me, and I had to turn my thoughts back to training mode and remember the techniques. The exhilaration of sailing through the air was excessively short. I prepared myself for the PLF — point of landing fall — and executed a smooth and otherwise anticlimactic landing on the ground.

I got up and watched the dotted sky as other paratroopers sailed to the ground, all calmly attached to their wide-open chutes. I then began the process of rolling up my chute and packing it into the carry bag. "Thank you, Lord, for being with me and seeing me through," I prayed audibly. My first big challenge was complete.

We had five jumps in all. The fifth took place on the final day of Airborne School. This last jump was followed by a brief ceremony where the commandant pinned brand-new silver wings on our chests. I was now officially a US Army paratrooper. The sweat running down my cheeks did not seem to be so bad at that moment. Did I feel like I had finally become a man and found my place after that first jump? You betcha! I was somebody! I smiled broadly, just thinking about it.

STANLEY COLEMAN
United States Army

As a new recruit in the United States Army in 1999, I chose NBC (Nuclear/Biological/Chemical) as my military occupational specialty (MOS). My recruiter led me to believe that I would be working in the study of defending against chemical warfare tactics. However, during my first three months in Korea, I found myself primarily being a lawn care maintenance technician (yard boy) for "happy mountains", aka, Korean graveyards, whenever I wasn't in the field. Nonetheless, I was extremely anxious to be able put my newly-acquired military skills to use at Camp Casey in South Korea.

Not recalling everything I'd learned during high school world history class concerning the Korean conflict, you can imagine my surprise at my first briefing when we were reminded that South Korea and North Korea were only at a cease-fire. Yet and still, this did not take away the excitement I had in anticipation of performing my NBC duties.

When I was assigned to my unit, 4th Chemical Company, I learned that my platoon was currently deployed to field exercises. It was the company's policy that all members of the platoon deploy together on all field exercises. This meant that upon arriving to South Korea, I only had the opportunity to spend one night in a bunk before joining my platoon in the field. Surprising to me, I was assigned to the smoke platoon. Smoke platoon is responsible for providing various methods of visual obscurant. In layman's terms, we created massive smoke screens that provided cover for friendly movement and to obscure the enemy's line of sight. The method of smoke distribution I used was through the M-58 smoke generator. This smoke generator is attached to a small tracked vehicle (tank). When a soldier first arrives to Korea as a "newbie", your job is to operate the smoke generator. Me being six-foot three, two hundred and thirty pounds, my accommodations were quite cramped, seeming as how the dimensions were approximately three feet by two feet.

Looking back, I think that an assignment in Korea is perfect for recently-graduated AIT soldiers. I say this because everyday operations are very similar to those soldiers' encounters in basic training and in AIT. I often thought, "man, I signed up for this," primarily because the tour of duty consisted of a year, and six months out of that year was spent in the field.

My second field exercise was scheduled for twenty-one days. During this time, we conducted personal hygiene using 32 oz. of hot water every other day. The smell was so overcoming until one could literally become lightheaded from the odor of their own body. The dirt in Korea had a familiar smell that you could never get used to, nor forget. You see, over there, they use human waste as fertilizer. Everywhere. So, you can imagine what that must have been like.

When we weren't in the field, we were training in the Garrison. In addition to training, we exercised quite strenuously. On Mondays, we ran 6-8 miles. Wednesdays, 4-6 miles, and Fridays 8-10. On Fridays, if you didn't complete the run with the company, you were restricted to the base for the entire weekend. During this time, I got to play a lot of Monopoly on base during the weekends at the USO.

Things did get serious during my tour once when a suspicious North Korean fishing boat was in restricted waters. You see, because the countries were only at a cease-fire, at a moment's notice, we could be at war. We were called on alert, issued our ammunition from the ammo supply point, and went to our fighting positions. One of the points made during our in-briefing, is how our artillery was pointed at strategic points in North Korea and the same goes for them to us.

It is always a serious situation when soldiers are called on alert and issued ammunition. During this time, it was very chaotic, exciting, and scary all at a same time. Because of my training, I was confident in my ability to do my part in the mission. This is not true for everyone, however. I was surprised to see a senior leader break down under the pressure and stress of what was going on and what could possibly happen.

I was equally amazed by how everyone kept going despite the situation that was going on with this particular leader. This was the day that I realized that I really was ready to fight and or die for my country. I imagine that everyone has this moment of reckoning when you have to carry out what you have been trained to do and it is a great feeling.

As chemical soldiers, we are one of a few combat support units that fight alongside female service members. I remember three females in our platoon who were highly capable of performing next to any service member, male or female. This is important to me because when it's time to fight, there is no more black, white, yellow, or brown, male or female, gay or straight. There is only American.

STEVE JURINA
United States Army

The year was 1998 and I was 17 years old. I had decided awhile back, and now I find myself wearing full fatigues, carrying an M16 A-2 rifle and marching on a hot Georgia road with other guys my age. This was Ft. Benning Georgia, home of the Infantry.

It was August and the humidity level was peaking 90% and at 94 degrees it might as well be 150! I was a few months into my Infantry training and we found ourselves following our Drill Sergeant at a brisk walk, 6 miles into a 10-mile trek, humping an 80-pound ruck. The sweat on my forehead felt like boiling water on my face and my feet were literally burning in my black combat boots.

I remember thinking to myself, "there's no way I'm going to make the rest of this march". I was toward the back of the line and following us on the road were several medvac humvees. A constant reminder that not everyone accomplishes this task. I kept visualizing myself in the back of one of those humvees, laying down under the cover of the canopy, getting fresh water. I kept hearing our Drill Sergeant yelling, 'faster, faster dammit!'. I started hearing what sounded like large bags of potatoes hitting the sandy gravel shoulder of the road. I started realizing that sound was my fellow soldiers falling out. More than likely suffering heat exhaustion or heat stroke. This was the hardest thing I've ever had to experience!

I felt like I was next. I wanted so badly to drop to the ground and give up. But, I remember counting my steps out loud. I don't exactly know why I was doing this, but it kind of made me feel like I had a goal, although I never actually set a particular number to count up to. I just kept counting.

I turned my head and looked back several times to see how many guys were getting IV's hooked up to them from the medvac unit people. There were several. Both lines of soldiers on both sides of the road were starting to thin out dramatically. Drill Sergeant continued to yell, 'Faster!'.

At this point we were all at almost double time. My feet hurt so bad and were literally on fire. Every time I took a breath, it felt like my lungs were taking in air from an oven. I slowly started to look up to the sky, resting my helmet against the top of my ruck giving me some relief to my aching head and neck. Why the hell did I sign up for this crap? I felt like death was knocking at my door and the further we marched, the more inviting death seemed over this hell.

I vaguely remember my Drill Sergeant yelling, '3 more miles, don't stop!'. Oh my God, 3 more miles. That really isn't that far, but it seems like a thousand miles when you're in this much pain. I still felt like I wasn't going to make it. Keep counting, keep counting. One two three ONE, one two three TWO, one two three THREE, one two three FOUR! As I was staring at the white clouds in the sky, my attention to my own counting became distracted by a small dark cloud in the distance.

I remember envisioning that small dark cloud growing rapidly and covering the sun from cooking us further and dumping rain. Oh, that would be such sweet relief! But, I know this is probably not going to happen. So, I closed my eyes and continued counting, matching my cadence with each step. Drill Sergeant yells out from the front, '2 more miles, step it up ladies, do not stop!'.

I suddenly notice my eyelids quit burning from the scorching sun. When I opened my eyes, I couldn't believe what I was witnessing. That small dark cloud had grown into a large dark cloud. This gave me hope to continue. And just in time, because I started to feel my knees buckle while I was marching. I started to fixate on the edge of the dark cloud and where the open sky met it. I knew in just a few seconds that edge would move away and reveal the damn sun again. And it did! Shit!

The heat seemed even worse than before. I think the small relief we got was too much to handle after having it. The sun, the heat, my feet, my sweat, my whole body felt like it was shutting down. I began to cry from the pain, but not out loud. That wouldn't be tolerated. I just couldn't handle it any longer. When is this pain going to stop? As my boiling tears were rolling down my face, something incredible, something divine, started happening. It started to sprinkle. You gotta be kidding me! This is great! I felt like I got a new wind. I reached up and dried my eyes and gritted my teeth. You can do this! You're almost done!

The Drill Sergeant yells out, '1 more mile, double time, double time'. Holy crap, anything but double time! Now we're running?! As I looked around me, I learned that my eyes weren't the only ones filled with tears. Everyone around me started grunting aloud. Almost animal like. Gritting their teeth and pushing through their pain. Soon we were all grunting, gritting and yelling our war cry!

I remember a soldier, about 4 people in front of me, was literally crying and yelling his war cry at the same time. Hell yeah! THAT is what this is gonna take to get through. At this point, an amazing thing took place, it started pouring down rain upon us. Pouring!

Before, we were running pathetically, gritting and yelling like wailing victims. Now? Now we were all running like we had a purpose, gritting and yelling as if we were thirsty for blood.

I felt a euphoric feeling overcome me. I don't know if it was the rain, or my adrenaline, but whatever it was my pain was no longer hindering my steps, it was fueling my fight. There's NO way I'm giving up. I got this!

I noticed the guys ahead of me in the line suddenly turned to the right, crossing the road and I followed. We had made it to Victory Hill. We were now running on soft green grass and what a beautiful relief it was.

We were quickly lined up in platoon formation. I took my place and we all ran in place yelling grunts and hugging each other and aggressively shaking each other's hands.

We did it, we made it! Then our Drill Sergeant yelled, 'Platoon, halt. Attention!'. We were all standing the best we could at attention, our chests rising and falling rapidly with the sound of everyone's hard breathing.

As we stood staring into oblivion, trying our hardest to fixate on our Drill Sergeant, I noticed that he had a slight smirk on his face. And then, the Drill Sergeant yelled our fight chant. This made it clear to us that we had made it, we had accomplished our mission. 'Echo two five four Infantry!', and in unison we all yelled with everything we had left in our lungs, 'FOLLOW ME!'. We came. We saw. We overcame. We conquered!

Today, I got my Infantry cross rifles pinned to my sweaty, dirty, rain soaked BDU top. A symbol signifying I was now part of an elite brotherhood; a brotherhood etched into American military history that has seen every major conflict and war this great country has fought. Today I am no longer 17 years old. Today...I am a soldier!

TRAVIS JOHNSON
United States Navy

When a high school teacher wanted to teach a class about privilege, he came up with a simple, but powerful and insightful object lesson for his students. At the beginning of the class, all the students received a piece of paper, and were asked to crumple it into a ball. Then, he moved the recycling bin to the front of the room. He told them, "the game is simple — you all represent the country's population. And everyone in the country has a chance to become wealthy and move into the upper class. To move into the upper class, all you must do is throw your wadded-up paper into the bin while sitting in your seat." The students in the back of the room immediately piped up and said it wasn't fair — the students in the front of the room obviously had a much better chance than they did.

All the students took their shots. Most of the students in the front of the room made it, and of course only a few students in the back of the room did. The teacher continued, "The closer you were to the recycling bin, the better your odds. This is what privilege looks like. Did you notice how the only ones who complained about fairness were in the back of the room? By contrast, people in the front of the room were less likely to be aware of the privilege

231

they were born into. All they can see is 10 feet between them and their goal."

Then the teacher wrapped things up with the most important thing to take away from this simple lesson: "Your job — as students who are receiving an education — is to be aware of your privilege. And use this particular privilege called 'education' to do your best to achieve great things, all the while advocating for those in rows behind you."

Starting in the back row can certainly be disheartening. When I talk to others about where I started in life, they can hardly believe I've achieved what I have. Some quick stats from my humble beginnings include: 47 moves; 12 schools before high school graduation; five foster homes; living with Mom, Grandma, and Dad; and getting in serious trouble with the law. Some would think we were living the American dream. We had multiple streams of income: welfare, child support, WIC, food stamps, social security, disability, and state assistance. The American dream, right?

Growing up I quickly understood that me and my situation was not like other kids and their situations. In northern Minnesota, it seemed, most kids lived in one house until graduation with their biological parents. I really had no idea what that was like. My parents were divorced since before I can remember. We lived outside of a small town, at the end of a gravel road, on a lake, in a trailer house. I can remember Mom calling my Dad over for a visit. A short time later the sheriff arrived just before my Dad and told him he wasn't welcome. What I was unaware of was that my Mom suffered from Bipolar Disorder and PTSD. Part of her mental illness included hallucinations. I'm sure she had envisioned my Dad coming to attack us, got scared, and called the sheriff. My Dad and I didn't develop a relationship until much later in life.

Mental healthcare in the 80s wasn't the best. The law reads that a person cannot be committed to a mental health institution unless that person is a danger to themselves or others. Although my Mom wasn't always in the best state-of-mind, she was never a physical threat to herself or others.

Life for my sister and I consisted of living with Mom, Mom getting sick and requiring treatment, and we moved. Sometimes we moved in with family members. Sometimes we were together. Sometimes we were apart. We'd get moved to a new school and moved back again when Mom was released from the hospital. Life was certainly stressful and this cycle began taking a toll on us. Grades were slipping and we were becoming hostile towards others. Not physically hostile, rather, apathetic and unapologetic. My sister began acting out and I started lying. I was lying about all sorts of things I'm embarrassed to admit to now. But life moved on.

This cycle became our norm, but I was getting older and fed up with the endless nonsense. I told my Mom that I was moving in with Grandma and that if she loved me, she would let me leave and not say a word about it. I was out! I had escaped the crazy. Grandma welcomed me in with open arms. I learned a great many lessons from my Grandma, including the importance of telling the truth, following through, and the value of hard work.

Despite being in the most stable environment I've ever lived in until then, I got in trouble with the law. Had I been older, I would be considered a felon and many of my options and opportunities would have vanished from my life. I barely knew right from wrong, and I almost screwed my future up over a few minutes I'd do nearly anything to take back. I was devastated, but not beyond hope. I made one of the top three decisions of my life. I chose to follow Jesus.

I graduated high school, but far from being an honor student. My unresolved stress had not been helpful in maintaining good grades. After high school, I worked two full time jobs and a part time job just to make ends meet. I was dating/living with my superhot girlfriend and inside a year, I had proposed. This is the second greatest decision of my life.

I remember talking to my Dad about my situation at the time. I told my Dad I wasn't making any money and I feared how I would support my future wife. He told me to get rid of all those crappy jobs and get one good job. He pitched the Navy and said they had some solid opportunities, but I should check them out for myself. I didn't really know much about the military other than they offered three hots and a cot. I knew I didn't want to be shot at; my life had been stressful enough already. I inquired at the Air Force recruiting station. Although they liked my ASVAB, they did not have room for someone with my criminal background. I talked to the Navy and they seemed to take a shine to me. Despite my criminal record, they said someone with my ASVAB should be able to obtain a waiver and join the Navy. I was excited, but I wasn't sure what job to take. My Dad said the Navy treats aviation boys pretty well. I made the next greatest decision of my life and joined the Navy as an Aviation Structural Mechanic (Safety Equipment). I signed up with a friend of mine, and together we told my fiancée the news. Surprisingly, she was on board with my decision and I left for boot camp soon thereafter.

The Navy represented a lot of things for me; opportunity and structure; a chance to prove myself without my family history clouding every topic; and my only likely path towards college. Boot camp and "A" school weren't easily accomplished, but I made it through. My first command was VFA-125 in NAS Lemoore, CA fixing ejection seats on the F/A-18. I quickly found the structure I was looking for. I also noticed the military was structured in a way that one could generate their own success. They told me exactly what they wanted me to do. When I finished that task or qualification, I asked for more. Apparently, this got my chain of command very excited. It's not often they have someone with that kind of motivation. I quickly got qualified in brake rider, duct diver, plane captain, daily, and was doing very well on my collateral duties. I also learned the difference between making mistakes as a civilian and as a military man. A quick side note, I had married my fiancée and returned to Lemoore.

I was working hard as the assistant Tool Petty Officer. I took the initiative to setup a new toolbox. Throughout this process, I broke a tool and threw it away. I finished my project, cleaned up, and went home. I was working Mid Check, which means I worked from 2200-0800. Around 1000, I received a call asking if I had worked on the tool box to which I replied yes. They asked what happened to the tools I was working with, the one that broke. I replied that I may have thrown it away. I then discovered that this was the absolute wrong thing to say. I was required to get my tail to work. Of course, I'm exhausted and my wife was at work with our only car. I ended up walking to the bus station, catching a ride to base, and getting on the base bus to catch a ride to the hanger. I was dog tired and not entirely sure what to expect. You see, accounting for tools in Naval Aviation is a big deal. With an unaccounted-for tool, all launches are cancelled until the tool is accounted for. I had not realized the gravity of my situation. Upon my arrival, I was again asked what happened. I fessed up and told them I threw the tool away. I was to jump in the dumpster and search for my mistake. I went to the dumpster and discovered that it had been emptied and there was nothing for me to search through. I reported to Quality

Assurance and made my statement about the incident. My punishment was to write 500 words on the importance of tool control by the following day. I was relieved because I knew the punishment could have been much more severe.

I turned in my paper to the Quality Assurance Officer. Upon reading my paper, he asked why I hadn't been straight up with him in the beginning. I replied that it wouldn't happen again. He was impressed with the quality of my paper and he expected more from me. Talking to my shop supervisor, he showed me the award they had written for my work on the tool box. Then he shredded it right before my eyes and replaced it with a counseling chit. I went from reward to punishment for not being up front and honest. Had I been apologetic and honest when they called me, they would have taken care of the paperwork and although I would have been talked to, I wouldn't have been in any serious trouble. The lesson: the sooner you man up to a mistake, the quicker the problem goes away.

I had done my fair share of detachments on the USS John C Stennis, USS Abraham Lincoln, USS Constellation, to NAS Fallon, NAS El Centro, NAS Key West, and JRB New Orleans. So, when it came time for the next detachment on the USS Constellation I was ready to go. My supervisor determined it was time to let some of the new guys get some boat experience. I was relieved for the break.

My phone rings, I check the clock...just before 0600, but it was my Dad so I answered. He asked what I was doing. I told him sleeping until the phone rang. He said to turn on the TV, don't argue just do it. I turned on the TV to see smoke rising from the first twin tower and by the time I asked what on earth was going on, the second plane impacted the second tower. My dad said two planes just impacted the world trade center and that we were under attack. My heart sank, and although I was in the Navy, I didn't really understand what that meant. My Dad said to go to work 4-5 hours early if I wanted any chance of getting to work on time. I was just glad that I wasn't on the ship or in New York for that matter.

He wasn't kidding. The line to get onto base stretched on for miles upon miles. They were doing a full search on each and every car going onto base, and no civilians were being granted access. I was the only one living off base to be to work on time. It, no kidding, took me over four hours to get there. The lesson: sometimes your Dad knows what he's talking about.

The panic following the attack eventually subsided. I found myself qualified as a Final Checker and to my knowledge, was one of only two airmen on base to have that qualification. My time was coming to a close at my first command. My wife was pregnant and I was up for orders. I asked my Dad what I should do and where should I go. He said that if I could see my child being born while on active duty, that I should choose to do so. This meant that I picked orders to VQ-4 on Tinker AFB near Oklahoma City, working on the E-6B Mercury.

The E-6 was not as exciting as the F-18, but it sure was a lot bigger. The E-6 is the largest jet in naval service. I was at the training command when I was notified that I had been promoted to Petty Officer Third Class. I was excited that my hard work paid off; and, with our first child on the way, the timing couldn't have been better. I had done what they told me to do and that resulted in outstanding evaluations. The lesson: doing what your boss needs results in more money in your pocket.

Once in VQ-4, I continued working hard and getting more qualifications to include my enlisted aviation warfare. This again resulted in a promotion just a short year after my last. I was now a Second-Class Petty Officer and they wanted me to be in charge of EVERYTHING. I quickly discovered that being in charge wasn't exactly as glamorous as it seemed. I was supposed to have all the answers...I barely had any. The number one thing I did know was that being the most qualified guy stunk. I went to work on getting my guys all the qualifications I had. The lesson: work is easier with everyone sharing the load.

My hard work did not go unnoticed. I was selected as an instructor for my next duty. I walked across the parking lot, got qualified to teach, and I studied my tail off for my next promotion. Once that exam was complete, I enrolled in college. That's right; it took me seven years to finally start college. I completed my Master Training Specialist and I started to become aware that my mouth was really off-putting. I didn't know the right words to say; so, I stopped talking in large groups unless I had something of value to add. I got promoted again and started receiving awards. Before it was all said and done, I was awarded three Navy and Marine Corps Achievement Medals while I was on instructor duty. The lesson: don't let your mouth get in the way of your good work.

My second child was born and I realized the chances of being promoted again, as an enlisted man, were pretty low, so I considered Officer Programs. After asking around and asking my Dad, I determined that if I had the desire then I should apply without delay. Many of the older sailors, my Dad included, said at some point they had the desire to apply but never actually finished the application process. And now, they were too old to qualify for any such program. I didn't want an opportunity like this to go to waste and I wasn't exactly a spring chicken myself, so I applied to the Seaman-to-Admiral Program.

The application process was no joke. They wanted to know everything about me. They wanted my evaluations, awards, ACT scores and so much more. I started comparing what I was submitting to others who submitted a package in the past. As far as I could tell, I was behind. Regardless, I kept the application process going. I had the full support of my wife and the command. A few months after getting all the information together, to include letters of recommendation and completing interview boards, I sent my application off to the selection board. A short five months later, my Officer in Charge called to notify me that I was selected as a Naval Flight Officer. The lesson: If you have the desire, work hard and go for it! If you don't apply, it's a guaranteed no.

I was off to do officer training, then on to college at the University of Oklahoma where I received my commission! Flight school was next and the hardest of all the tasks I had completed up until that point. I selected orders back to fly the E-6 and was stationed at VQ-3. After more qualifications, I was again selected to instruct the next generation.

I was as far from being privileged as anyone I had ever met. Through a few amazing choices, following Jesus, diligence and perseverance, I could get a great job, marry a wonderful woman, have two beautiful children, and serve the community in which I live. It's not about where you start, but how you react to all the things outside of your control. How you roll with the punches, dust yourself off, gain wisdom and direction, and move forward. My wife and I are debt free, minus the house, and spend our time mentoring others. Now that we are at or near the front row, we must not forget those in rows behind us.

MARK SWEENEY
United States Airforce

It was a quiet afternoon in the Sheet Metal Mechanic shop at Yokota Air Force Base Japan, until. "Jackson, come here quick." I heard someone yell. I turned to see who it was and my boss was walking in the door with another Non-Commissioned Officer. "Come here Jack" he yelled. I ran over to see what was wrong. "Jack, I need a piece of tubing ASAP!" Tubing is what spreads fluids throughout an aircraft. In the work field of Aircraft Structural Maintenance, we perform all kinds of work on airplanes. From replacing cracked or missing metal on wings to replacing the smallest fastener in the hardest to reach place. We also create and fix the cracked or damaged tubing inside aircrafts.

So, I asked how long and how wide the tubing needed to be. When he described it to me I knew we were in trouble. I could also tell, "We don't have that, sir." was not what he wanted to hear by the panicked look both of their faces. "Jack, I need that tubing, 5 minutes ago" he said hurriedly. "Can you make it for me?" I replied yes sir and ran out the door. Now I'm sure that wasn't what he expected but I felt in my bones that I'd seen a large piece of tube that I could cut down for him at our paint shop.

So, I ran over to the paint shop which was actually 5 buildings away. Running as fast as I could I burst into the door of the paint shop. "Jack where is the fire man?" I heard one of my friends say as I sprinted past him. "Yo! Jack, slow down man." I heard another one of them say as he was painting wing part. "Is that piece of tubing still in the metal room?" I yelled back at him still in stride. "Yeah" he replied.

Opening the door to the metal room I could see the tube leaning against the wall. I grabbed it quickly and began my sprint back to the shop. Running as fast as possible I yelled "Like this?" entering the shop door. "Yes, but shorter." they replied at the same time. So, I proceeded to the Tube cutter, now this machine needed some assembly so I completed quickly, pulse racing and heart still pumping from all the running. Slicing through the metal I cut the tube down to perfect size. Once complete I took a moment to sand the edge smooth to prevent cracking. "Here you go sir." "Thanks Jack you are a life saver." "No problem sir." and then they left just as fast as they showed up.

I went on with my day, weeks past and I forgot all about that day until one morning during roll call. "Airman Jackson step forward." I looked at my fellow airmen like and stepped up to the front. "Airman Jackson we would like to present you with the award Maintenance Professional of the Month. A few weeks ago, I came in here and asked Jack to cut me a piece of tubing. I didn't tell him what it was for because I wasn't allowed to at the time. He didn't ask questions. Also, when he saw that what I needed wasn't here he did not make excuses or give up. He ran all the way to paint shop to get what I needed.

He cut the tube, gave it to me, and kept on working. What he didn't know and neither did any of you was this.

That day, one of our aircraft had major damage and was leaking fluids badly. Normally these fluids are drained into a large hole in the floor but the part of the plane that does this was damaged. If we were to open it the fluid would not have drained into the floor but spilled all over causing a huge hazardous waste spill. Jack that tube you made allowed us to drain the fluid from the place a prevent the leak. But here is the most important part. That plane was carrying Air Force VIP's and their families. We can't say who the VIP's are because those people fly into the base top secret. Which is why we couldn't even tell you what the tube was for. The liquid that was leaking is highly flammable, if we wouldn't have had the tube you ran to find all outcomes were going to be bad. Today we honor you and this is a reminder to all of you. No matter how small the job, give it your all. You never know who it will impact. It's the little things."

I was amazed that something as small as a piece of tubing could have such a huge impact. That event went on to have a huge impact on my career. Because I won Maintenance Professional of the Month, I was able to win Airman of the Year for the Air Force. I then received an early promotion because I received both of those awards in one year. All form just doing one little thing. One little thing had grown to benefit me and others.

In life, we never know what one little thing we do will grow into the greatness the have always dreamed of. We never know what one little thing could save someone's life. Everyday veterans and military members commit suicide. Who knows if one little thing you do today could save that one life that needed to be saved. What if you, taking the time to ask, "Is everything ok?" is the little thing that keeps that person alive today because you showed them someone cared when they thought no one did. What if spending a few minutes with a person you can tell is depressed and just listening to them, is the one little thing that saves their life because they believe no one ever listens to how they feel. What if?

What if? You notice them giving away their possessions or you notice someone trying to hurt himself in a small way possibly some cuts. Noticing that little thing could help you identify someone who is thinking of dying before it happens. You could save a life by doing or notice just one little thing.

So, remember that THE LITTLE THINGS ARE THE BIG THINGS. As my boss to me the day I received my award "No matter how small the job, give it your all. You never know who it will impact. It's the little things."

MATTHEW WHITTINGTON
United States Marines

Gravelly asphalt drones under the tires of my Dad's old farm truck as we traverse the back roads of Toppenish Washington toward the first field of the day. I've managed to roll down my window; the aromas of mint, hops and my Dad's coffee fill my nostrils. Looking out the window as far as my four-year-old eyes can see are the rolling hills of the Yakima Valley and the young crops of summer. I marvel over the flow of water through the canals, it is only this time of year that the canals flow and for the first time they have my attention. My mind does not yet understand why, but I know the relentless powerful flow of the water makes my Dad happy. It's as if the water is his compass as we follow it along roads and through the fields.

I look down at the bench seat and see my Scooby Doo lunch pail. It's not as big and grown up as my Dad's thermos and black plastic lunch box with cool metal clamps, yet I proudly clutch its handle all the same. Today is special. Today I will not be commanding my airplane made from the upside-down coffee table placed on the couch so that my mom can vacuum. I will not be spending the day with Grandma either. No, today I am working with Dad!

246

As if sensing I have flown elsewhere Dad pulls me back to Earth with his voice, "Matthew, count to 25 for me." Dutifully I reel off the numbers and take great satisfaction in the glowing smile below that bushy mustache. His cheeks and chin are covered in black stubble, I ponder a conversation had just moments ago it seems when I had asked him why I didn't get to watch him mix shaving cream in the cup with trains on it. "We need to get on the road son, the fields need water" he had said. As if on que we glide to a stop and Dad says, "Let's go son."

I climb out of the truck and follow my father to the tailgate. He lowers the tailgate with a thud and begins placing irrigation tubes on the ground. They seem ponderously heavy as I note the veins bulging in his biceps and forearms. I ask to help lift them. Dad responds kindly, yet denies me the opportunity to help with the lifting. Instead, he points to the first landing yards away and assigns my first mission of the day. "Son, start there and count off 25 rows." Giddy with excitement and proud to be helping my Dad I count off; 1...2...3...and so on until without error my feet stop at 25. I look behind and with deft expertise my Dad's irrigation tubes have brought water to each row I had counted out for him. Accomplishment and awe well up, I beam as the water slowly flows and serpentines around dirt clods filling the neatly laid rows.

Feeling a job well done I say, "Now what Dad?" Sensing my pride and perhaps sensing what lays ahead in his young boy's life he smiles and responds with the simplest and most profound of answers, "Keep counting son, 25 more."

***

It's early spring of 1993 and I'm sitting at my Papa's dining room table in Everett Washington. I had just finished mowing his yard and eating a peanut butter and grape jelly sandwich with apple juice my Nana had made. My Papa sits at the head of the table and I am seated to his right. My junior year of high school is coming to an end and Papa wants to discuss my future. When my Papa spoke, I listened, his persona demanded that respect. I had only a few years prior done a story board in school for the culture fair and the subject was my family history in the military. My Dad's father was an Army Veteran of World War 2, I knew very little about him since he had died when my Dad was a teen. My Dad served in the Army, 101st Airborne in Vietnam. My Papa served in the Navy, specifically the Pacific Theater on the USS Ommaney Bay. Early in 1945 shortly after transiting the Surigao Strait into the Sulu Sea, a twin engine Japanese suicide plane penetrated the fleet undetected and headed for the Ommaney Bay. The plane clipped the island and crashed into the flight deck on the forward starboard side. Bombs carried by the suicide plane released; one penetrated the flight deck and detonated below, setting off a series of explosions among fully fueled planes on the hangar deck. The second bomb passed through the hangar deck, ruptured the fire main on the second deck then exploded.

Forward water pressure, power and bridge communications were all immediately lost. The ensuing inferno and thick black smoke quickly made it impossible to fight the fires. Escort ships were not able to lend power to the fight due to exploding ammunition, incredible heat temperatures, and stored torpedo warheads that were thought to be exploding imminently. The order to abandon ship was given at 1750. At 1945 the carrier was sunk by a torpedo from the Destroyer Burns. In total 95 sailors lost their lives, my Papa had to swim for his life since rescue boats couldn't get too close.

Papa looks me square in the eyes, without much small talk he wants to know what I'm going to do upon graduation. He notes my near 4.0 GPA through high school, and gives slight acknowledgment of that accomplishment, but Papa really wants to make sure that the hard work I put into school isn't wasted. I tell him that I want to be a fighter pilot. He seems pleased to hear of my aspirations. Papa asked me what I wanted to fly and I said F/A – 18 Hornets in the Navy. Given his Navy career and the pride I'd seen from him over the years when discussing his fellow Ommaney Bay survivors, I had expected that my desire to fly Hornets off carriers would please him.

Understandably he was not dismissive, but rather he said, "That would be a fine choice and the Navy would be good for you, but why not the Marines?" Frankly I'd put no thought into the Marine Corps at that point. Confused, I asked my Papa, who only ever talked about the Navy, "Why the Marines?" His response was simple, yet I will not forget its impact or simplicity for the rest of my life. Papa said, "Matthew, I've watched you be prideful and want perfection in everything you do; from your academics, to your baseball and even the work you've done. Nobody is more prideful, nobody does it better than the Marines." Sold!

***

A few weeks after the conversation with my Papa I drove from Arlington Washington to the Marine Corps recruiting office in Everett. I didn't notify my parents, I didn't tell anybody of my plans. I didn't consider so much as even giving courtesy visits to the Navy, Army, or Air Force. Papa had convinced me; my personality was a perfect fit for the Marines. I walked into the recruiter's office and a few Marines were sitting around desks. The man who spoke to me first was a Sergeant whose name I don't recall. He asked what I wanted to do, and I told him that I'm going to fly. Regarding all of what was said after that I remember very little. The recruiter had me take some tests, I scored well enough that he told me, "With your intelligence you can do anything you want. You said you want to fly. I can't enlist you to be an Officer, but I can sign you up to enlist and you can go be an Officer after you're already in." At the time, I was a little naïve and it all sounded good. He asked what I wanted to enlist to do; I chose Aircraft Mechanic since that was exactly what my Papa had done 50 years prior. Since I still had a senior year to get through the recruiter signed me up for a delayed entry contract. Essentially my senior year counted as my first year of inactive reserve duty, I would do six years active instead of four and in exchange for the two extra years I got an automatic promotion upon boot camp graduation and choice of which coast I'd be stationed on: East, West or Japan. I chose California.

Senior year of high school while in delayed entry was a little surreal. What I mean by that is it seemed to me there was little purpose in going at all. I already knew where I was going upon graduation, within two weeks of my diploma I'd be at MCRD San Diego. I elected that in lieu of sports, especially baseball which I loved very much, I'd instead work out in preparation for boot camp and work part time to have a little fun before I left. To nobody's surprise I still maximized grades because I wanted to graduate with honors and strengthen my case to be selected for ROTC.

On January 7, 1994, I was sitting in my first class of the day, AP English with Mr. Cleeves. Someone from the office paged me over the intercom to report to the Vice Principals office. When I got to the office my mom was on the phone and she was crying, my Papa had died.

I was in shock. My Papa, Jack Edward King, gone.

The funeral was a few days later, the graveside service was at Evergreen Funeral home in Everett Washington. The service was beautiful and powerful, but what struck me the most was when a sailor in full white stood 10-20 yards up the hill from his resting place and blew the most beautiful and sad notes I'd ever heard on a trumpet, Taps.

Marine Corps boot camp was six short months away. I attended a number of monthly recruiter activities leading up to the spring; PFTs (Physical Fitness Tests), pick up football games, learning to field strip M-16s, etc. During the Spring, I ran 3 miles a few times each week on uneven terrain and hills then lifted weights at the high school. I talked to my recruiter more about being an Officer and he arranged for me to do a PFT and interview for ROTC. On the day of the PFT they had me run around Green Lake in Seattle, they told me that I ran it in 20 minutes. After the run is when they had me do the sit ups and pull ups. Sit ups came first and I did 75 in 2 minutes then finished by doing 12 dead hang pull ups. My academic record stood out to the interviewer, and then he asked me if I'd done any community service and I told him no. I told the interviewer about the part time job I'd had since I was 16, the baseball team, and the strength of classes

I had taken for my 3.97 GPA like Advanced English and Physics. I thought I'd nailed the interview. My recruiter called a few weeks later to inform me that ROTC had rejected me due to not enough pull ups and community service.

High school graduation came and went; I wanted no graduation gifts since I was leaving in a few weeks. I didn't celebrate any more than a barbeque with my family in the back yard. It all seemed anti-climactic to me and the Marine Corps loomed large on the near horizon. I was starting to get nervous due to the unknown and frankly still a little dejected at the ROTC rejection. I spent the last few weeks of civilian life unremarkably.

***

June 25, 1994. The recruiter pulls into our driveway in the afternoon in his gray government Ford Taurus. There is conversation with my parents about what to expect, when they'll hear from me, and that he would try to keep them updated. I don't recall anybody really crying much, which was probably a good thing for my state of mind, I'm sure my parents did after I left. The ride to Seattle was quiet, I didn't talk much. The recruiter told me to go into training trying to stand out and be a badass, I found it funny. My dad had advised I be quiet and just do what I'm told. He checked me into a motel down by Seattle Meps where I tried to sleep, but got very little due to the early wake up coming and all the other people partying in the hallways. The next day I was screened by doctors seemingly all day. I took my oath on June 26, 1994 and on a plane I went.

The plane landed in San Diego at night. There was a bus outside with a Marine standing next to it. He had a list of who he was expecting, my name was checked off and on the bus I went. The wait for the bus to fill up seemingly took all night. Nobody said a word. Eventually the driver was satisfied he'd had everybody he needed; the trip to MCRD was short and dead quiet. The bus came to a stop, the doors opened and a drill instructor stepped onto the bus and issued orders on how to get off the bus and where to stand.

Yellow footprints. Our feet had to match the yellow footprints. Heels touching and toes at a 45-degree angle. We were not to talk unless spoken to, how loud to respond when spoken to, we were told how to move, how quickly to move, how to sit, when to urinate, and how quickly to eat. The first few days were such a blur at MCRD. The first thing I remember after the yellow footprints in the middle of the night was getting all my hair cut off which happened in less than 20-30 seconds. They buzz it right off just like you see in the movie Full Metal Jacket. After that I remember being stripped of my civilian clothes; in my case blue jeans and a baseball mock turtle neck. They issue plain utility clothes, a cover (hat), and boots. The first days you are in what amounts to an administrative platoon. More medical screening, LOTS of immunizations LOTS of needles and a whole lot of sitting in line "A to B" on the ground waiting to be seen. You fill out what seems like endless paperwork for their jacket on you, and back in 1994 each page had to have your social security number on it. The whole screening process took about two days I think. I say I think because in Marine Corps Basic Training you lose track of the date, the days, and lots of hours. I kept track of my days by just trying to make it to the next meal.

The day finally came. The drill instructor marching us through all of that screening told us we were being turned over to our training platoons. I was placed with Alpha Company Platoon 1030. Senior Drill Instructor Staff Sergeant Becerra. We were taken to the squad bay where we would be sleeping and learning hygiene and stood in rows facing each other at the end of bunks, just like you see in Full Metal Jacket. In walks the Senior Drill Instructor followed by his Drill Instructors; Sergeants Crane, Cullen, and Buck. He says a few words to us about what is going to happen, his mission, and what he expects from us "Recruits." He turns to his Drill Instructors, they take vows about our training and then…he turns them LOOSE.

I would be lying if I tried to give a moment by moment account of what it's like to have Marine Drill Instructors unleashed on you for the first time, but it goes something like this. There is a whole lot of yelling and screaming about everything you could possibly imagine and some things you could not imagine. You could expect to hear yelling about the angle of your feet in relation to your heels. You are getting yelled at for your thumbs not being properly aligned with the seam of your trousers and other knuckles. You are getting yelled at if you one time forget to say 'Sir" as the first and last words out of your mouth. You are especially getting torn up if you let your eyes wander or snicker at another recruit getting yelled at. And that is hard, I will tell you some of those Drill Instructors are damn funny.

After the initial shock and awe barrage of Drill Instructors they get you outside and teach you how to form up into a formation to get from point to point. You go *everywhere* in formation. To the chow hall, to class, and especially to get your asses kicked in the sand pits. When I say getting your ass kicked, we're not talking actual assault here, though at times I thought it sounded preferable. What I'm talking about is thrashing PT until your breaking point of exhaustion. Side straddle hops (jumping jacks), flutter kicks, pushups, sit ups, and run in place "HIGH KNEES HIGH KNEES." It was in one of these sand pits with no end in sight that I first witnessed and felt utter despair and a creeping self-doubt about my ability make it through Marine Recruit Training. What you don't realize until you're out there is that the Recruit Depot shares a fence with San Diego Airport. All day while you're out there getting thrashed and marching on that blazing parade deck people are flying away, out of town right over your head. The thought creeps in, *"Why am I not on that plane?"* So, it was in one of these first days that one of my fellow recruits made a break for the fence. He was quickly tackled by one of the drill instructors and I never saw him again. The message I took, there is no escape.

It doesn't take long as a Marine Corps recruit to be humbled, no matter how much you worked out before, how much you ran, no matter how good of shape you think you're in the time comes when you are humbled. My time happened maybe a week in. Platoon 1030 was out by the obstacle course working out by lifting logs as a team. Following the exhaustive work with logs Drill Instructor Crane took us to the rope. Many recruits were able to climb the rope all the way up, yet when it was my turn I was still so exhausted from the logs I made it about three quarters of the way up and could not continue. Sergeant Crane was screaming at me, "Recruit get up that rope!" I had reached full muscle fatigue and could not. I slid down the rope in utter defeat and demoralization to Sergeant Crane losing his mind screaming at me. I won't lie, I wanted to quit. I wanted to board one of those planes and fly home. I felt lied to by my recruiter. I felt alone. I saw no way through, no end in sight. I made it through the rest of the day and the best part of the day finally came, the Drill Instructor's order to "Sleep recruit." I lay there in my bottom rack, I wanted to cry. My muscles ached and there were blisters on my feet and I knew, it was only going to be a few short hours until reveille and we'd do it all again. The sun went down and I caught glimpse of a flash out the squad bay window. I turned my head and looked, it was fireworks. The day was July 4, 1994 and I was watching fireworks over San Diego. My favorite holiday as a kid was Independence Day. My dad would buy tons of fireworks from the reservation and we'd spend all day lighting off firecracker cans, bottle rockets and the like before finishing the night with those balls that went into tubes for the colorful stuff. Independence Day and I am anything but independent. I cried. The timing of what would happen next was so profound that it still grips my emotions to this day, Taps. Taps played right then under the fireworks. My mind washed over what those notes meant and the sacrifices that had been made long before me. The fight for life my dad suffered in the worst years of Vietnam. My Papa's fight for life as the Ommaney Bay sunk and his fellow sailors died there in the Sulu Sea while he swam to rescue. All the generations of American Servicemen who preceded me and would follow me, surely, I could survive 12 more weeks of Marine Recruit training. It was in those moments my resolve solidified and my determination to succeed and not be broken grew. It was that night, alone in my bunk under fireworks and Taps, that I said to myself: In moments of weakness, I will internalize

Taps. I will not let my Papa, my dad, or myself down. I will be a United States Marine.

THANK YOU!

Thank you for reading these stories. It is my hope that they have encouraged you to reach out to even more veterans and learn their stories.

Thank you, Veterans. For your service, and for sharing your stories with all who will read them. Your willingness to share helps so many – it helps other veterans to know they are not alone, and it helps civilians have a better understanding of your internal world. You have also helped yourselves, by writing out so many stories you may not have thought about in many years.

Thank you to those who have purchased this book. You are supporting veterans, you are supporting the Books By Vets project, and you are supporting Hooves for Heroes. A percentage of all profits from the sale of this book are donated to Hooves for Heroes – an equestrian therapy program for veterans.

For more information about Books By Vets and the Veterans who contributed to Walk with Warriors – A Journey of Heroes, please visit www.booksbyvets.org. To contact the author, Shannon Whittington, regarding speaking opportunities or other events, please email booksbyvets@gmail.com.